A Way Through

Louise Gourlay

Copyright © 2017 Louise Gourlay

All rights reserved, including the right to reproduce this book, or portions thereof in any form. No part of this text may be reproduced, transmitted, downloaded, decompiled, reverse engineered, or stored, in any form or introduced into any information storage and retrieval system, in any form or by any means, whether electronic or mechanical without the express written permission of the author.

The views expressed in this work are solely those of the author and do not necessarily reflect the views of the publisher, and the publisher hereby disclaims any responsibility for them.

Cover photo by Jago Gourlay

ISBN: 978-0-244-04661-3

PublishNation
www.publishnation.co.uk

PREFACE

I have always been uncomfortable with the word 'journey' but can simply find no better word to describe what has been exactly that. I started writing a diary about five months after my second diagnosis of cancer. Since then, over the past three years, I have abandoned and revisited many times what has eventually ended up as a book.

The real reason for writing was born out of frustration with a medical system and a society which seem to promote fear, helplessness and often despair for cancer patients, especially those of us labelled as 'incurable' or 'terminal'. I knew from my own research that many people were healing themselves naturally from cancer or living a good life with cancer way beyond their prognoses. These people were getting well by making often significant changes to their physical, mental, emotional and spiritual health. I knew I could get well too and wanted to learn from them. As I worked my way through the mental and emotional turmoil that existed in my life before a recurrence of cancer, I began to see clearly and find immense peace and happiness. I realised that the right mindset is critical in order to heal and so my real hope for this book is to give others the hope, courage and determination, alongside practical tools and information, to find their own way to better health. I want readers to become aware of their own potential and inner wisdom for healing – to realise that each of us is different and may, therefore, need to focus on different aspects of our health. They are all connected, so as we work on one aspect, others will be affected but they all need attention.

Towards the end of the writing process, though, I realised that there was another really important message I wanted to convey. I had managed to transform my outlook and way of thinking, which showed me how to live life from a magical and fresh perspective. As this happened, my desperate need to be cancer free softened as I realised that I had never been happier than I was and am, living with cancer. I do have a strong conviction that I will be 'cancer free' one day – I can feel it in my bones (excuse the pun as that is where the cancer returned) – but healing your life and curing a disease are not the same thing, and although I would like and am expecting both, I know which one is more important. I hope that readers will learn the importance of finding happiness and making ourselves whole (healed), and be aware of a mindset that obsesses about disease and how to be rid of it, thus missing out on life in the process.

I have done exactly that on and off over the past three years. It has been a massive struggle at times, and now, further along my journey, I can be inclined to forget just how hard it has been at times, mentally, emotionally and physically. I have been so lucky to have the support of an incredible man, my husband, who has taught me so much about love and what matters. It is so simple and I had made it so complicated. Thank you, Robbie, for being my biggest teacher and my dearest friend.

So whatever your challenge and whatever stage of that challenge you are at, if you want to reach a better place in your life and your health and are willing to change, it is my biggest hope that this book will help you, at least a little. I have written it for you.

INTRODUCTION

I first set out to write a book that would provide the sort of guidance I would have liked when I was diagnosed with stage IV, advanced breast cancer in 2014 – a sort of 'first port of call' of information to help people understand and implement the basic changes needed to begin regaining their health. It would include all the things that are more or less universally accepted as beneficial to us all and essential in recovering from cancer. It would also condense and clarify the huge amount of information out there, that is confusing at the best of times. I wanted, first and foremost, to provide a message of hope and explain that we need not be so fearful of cancer and that many people are making remarkable recoveries, some of which are fast and some of which take longer. Cancer, I believe, is reversible, even with a poor prognosis and testimonials abound to prove this if you search for them. However, our present understanding around this disease is often limited and the information available can be unhelpful. We give it so much power, whilst we give our ability to address it so little.

In the process of writing, however, I was taken on a journey of self-discovery, which has meant pulling away at the layers of confusion, chaos and negativity which had taken hold of my mind, until finally I was able to find immense clarity and a sense of peace. What I have ended up with, in my writing, is a collection of reflections and suggestions. They are the advice and encouragement I would have liked to have had and the companion to a journey we so often go on when confronted by any event that turns our lives upside down. There may seem to be a fair amount of repetition within the book, but that is as a result of the interconnectedness of the different components of our health – the physical, mental, emotional and spiritual aspects that make us whole.

The message really is that only we can create wellness for ourselves as we are the only ones who will ever know ourselves properly. Of course we can use a doctor, medicine or anything we choose to help us but change comes from within, so that is where we need to go. It will involve us learning to gain a lot more self-awareness and to reconnect with who we really are, so that we can restore the balance we have lost in ourselves. We can learn how to start taking care of ourselves and what, ultimately, we need to change in our lives to bring about that balance.

Until we start to deal with our mental and emotional health, we will not unlock the enthusiasm and determination to take on the challenge of life, and therefore our chances of healing our physical health, let alone our lives, will be reduced. There may be issues from the past we need to deal with and often we need to learn how to let go of stress (especially with a cancer diagnosis) and experience life differently. Having good mental and emotional health means living our lives in our own unique way. It means loving and accepting ourselves rather than beating ourselves up about everything and trying to be perfect. A cancer diagnosis is the perfect catalyst to sorting out our lives and starting to live the life we want to. We just need a bit more common-sense, calm and understanding as we travel this road.

As I began writing it became clear that my physical recovery from cancer was inextricably linked to my efforts to tackle my mental health and my ability to handle stress, which had gradually been affecting my joy of life. This, my second diagnosis, made me face the realisation that I had been overly anxious and mildly depressed for much of my life, and that I had to do something about it if I wanted to live.

I have been searching all my life for something and some meaning, and it is only through this experience of illness that I have learnt how to find peace and stillness within me. I had been living for years unable to see a bright future even though I had an incredible amount to be grateful for. Staring death in the face made me realise how badly I wanted that future and that I would do anything to get there. That determination has led me to research and learn as much as possible about the human mind and the effect it has on our lives, and to learn how to change my thoughts so that I experience life differently.

What I have learnt is that we can control how we think, which affects how we feel, which in turn affects our lives. Not only can we live more enjoyable and meaningful lives by choosing better thoughts but we can change the entire reality of our lives. We can do this when we move from reacting to our lives and problems, to becoming the creative force in our lives, shaping the things and future that we want.

Mental and emotional wellbeing are the areas of our health that are so neglected and that are crucial to recovery. They are the missing link in the long and not particularly successful 'war on cancer' that the medical world, media and big charities have been fighting for years now. Paramahansa Yogananda (Indian yogi and guru) said,

"Whatever you hold in your mind will be produced in the physical body...Worry and stress have caused new deadly illnesses, such as high blood pressure, heart troubles, nervous breakdowns and cancer. All diseases have their origins in the mind".

Our minds can help or hinder our recovery, and our experience of life in general. By listening to our emotions more, we learn to use them as indicators of how we are doing. When we feel good, all is well, but when we don't, we need to find ways of making ourselves feel better by doing things we love or thinking better thoughts. If we are really struggling to find anything good about our current reality, then we need to turn to our imaginations. This may sound both too simplistic and hard, but it is just a matter of trying to change a repetitive cycle or way of thinking that has become a habit for many of us. We need to focus not on cancer but on wellbeing and do what feels right for ourselves - body, mind and soul. A trust in something greater than ourselves, in life itself, can help us replace anxiousness with peace and fear with hope, as we learn that sometimes we just need to let go and trust things will work out. When we really do this, things so often do.

It is a cliché, but like many before, I am grateful for the whole experience that chronic illness has given me, for that last chance to learn to live fully and to really value myself, those that I love and the magical, mystical world around me. Cancer has nourished my will to live and I am grateful for it. There is so much more to the world than we know, and I think that gradually, more and more of us will understand that we can find our own path to physical and emotional wholeness. We can use the help of a doctor, conventional medicine, a special diet, meditation or a combination of different things. There are so many ways to support ourselves on our way to regain our health. Whatever gives us peace of mind will help us.

I am 'work in progress'. I know life will bring more challenges my way, whether they be health related or not. I know I can handle them and so can you. Take it one day at a time and remember that when one door closes, another always opens. Life is to be lived now, not to be put on hold until the disease has gone. It is how we choose to live our life which really matters and will more often than not help determine our outcome.

One thing I know for sure is that we do have a choice as to how we live our lives, and when we open our hearts and minds, and start living our lives as boldly, joyfully and lovingly as we can, knowing that anything is possible, we will be awakened to a whole new way of living.

> *"It is only in our darkest hours that we may discover the true strength of the brilliant light within ourselves that can never, ever, be dimmed".*
> **Doe Zantamat** (author, artist and photographer)

A PERSONAL HISTORY

I was diagnosed with breast cancer in March 2008, at the age of thirty-eight, after eight months of being told the lump on my breast was a cyst. I had three children aged five, seven and nine. I had a mastectomy followed by six months of routine chemotherapy. I had bad side effects and my hair fell out. I was very scared initially and terrified of dying early, leaving my children and husband behind. Afterwards though, I got on with my life.

I had had the strong realisation soon after my diagnosis that this was a wake-up call and that I needed to make big changes to my life. I had given up work and was struggling with that. Even though I obviously adored my children and did love being with them, I felt really guilty for not working or, in my eyes, contributing anything to the world. Of course I knew that bringing up my children to the best of my ability was the most important thing I could do, but I still couldn't stop these nagging feelings around not working. I wanted so badly to do something positive and help make changes to problems I saw everywhere. I had so many ideas floating around in my head, but never had the confidence to put any of them into action. I continued as a full-time mother, volunteering in various projects here and there but feeling increasingly guilty, worthless and frustrated. To add to that, I never did anything for myself. I didn't place any importance on my own needs – they were bottom of the pecking order. I knew I needed to sort my head out and find some clarity amongst my confusion and endless searching, but I didn't do anything about this so completely ignored the promise I had made to myself to sort things out.

Then late in 2013 I started having severe pain in my hip. The doctor thought it might be a sports injury related to the little bit of running I did with my dogs, but the pain continued and soon I was hobbling around, finding it increasingly hard to walk. Eventually I pushed for an MRI scan, which confirmed that I had numerous metastases to my bones – too many to count. Further tests showed I had three lung nodules. I was told I had stage *IV* incurable breast cancer and that I probably had only a few years to live. The doctor told me she had had a good cry when she saw the results and I took little comfort from that.

I knew that I hadn't changed one thing about my life since my first diagnosis. I knew that my diagnosis in 2008 had been nature's way of getting me to stop, listen and change things. I hadn't though and here it was again, but even more real, raw and terrifying. I was pushed down the road of treatment very quickly and felt out of control, but then I started searching...for stories of hope, miracles and information that would help me to make the changes that might prolong my life.

Thus began a journey that I believe many people go on be it through illness, bereavement, depression or any sort of challenging time, which has taught me to truly live. There was no alternative really, as far as I was concerned, except to change how I thought and live, or die young and full of regret. I knew I had been living with a mind that controlled me and didn't serve me in the slightest and I knew I needed to change that. I just didn't know how exactly.

The first week after diagnosis was so terrifying. I couldn't allow my thoughts to dwell on the fact that I wouldn't be there as my children grew up, wouldn't be there to comfort and support them when things were tough and wouldn't be the wonderful grandmother I planned to be. Then there was my husband – my kind, gentle husband who had loved me so unconditionally and sometimes undeservedly throughout our time together. I remember going to watch a film with a good friend. I was an emotional mess and made myself go, but I could only think of my husband at home. In my mind, I saw him in the arms of a lovely, pretty girl - happy and in love, and although I honestly felt some joy in this, that at last he would have what he deserved, I felt a deep sense of loss. It should be me there and he should have been given that love from me during our time together. I so desperately wanted time to give him back the love he should have received from me.

I drove home howling, swearing and furiously angry for the first time since the diagnosis the week before. I have never witnessed, let alone performed, such an outburst of intense emotion before or since. We had not yet told our children of the diagnosis and it was hard trying to behave normally whilst the whole drama was unfolding. I rushed home to him, sobbing my heart out and a few minutes after comforting me he was showing me some meat stew recipe he liked the look of in the paper he was reading. Little did he know what was in store for him on the food front, and that meat stew would be off the menu for a while! He always had two feet firmly on the ground – a rock amongst the mental and emotional chaos I was living in, yet full of empathy, understanding and wisdom when I needed it.

I went for a second opinion in London and was rushed in for more tests and scans. I had mysteriously gone deaf in my left ear and there was no understanding as to why. The oncologist was worried it was in my nervous system. He was fairly sure the cancer had mutated and was no longer the same type as the original, which was hormonal. I was very, very scared and I remember him telling me that I was an 'unusual' cancer patient and he wanted me to be a 'normal' one. A lumbar puncture confirmed the good news that it wasn't in my nervous system but a biopsy confirmed his suspicion that it was no longer fed by oestrogen and was now triple negative, which I was told is harder to treat as they are unsure as to what feeds it. He concluded that the deafness was linked to cancer – paraneoplastic syndrome which has something to do with tumour cells excreting a substance and attacking the body. I also had three small indeterminate lung nodules. I started five daily sessions of radiotherapy to help with the pain in my hip area and was then rushed in to start chemotherapy.

The entire period was steeped in fear, yet somehow, being faced with my own mortality, I began to find an enormous strength and will to live, and for the first time in many years, a kindness and love towards myself. I made a promise there and then that I would change this time, that I would put my life in order and find out how to take care of all aspects of my health. I remember walking in the woods and making a pact with the universe…I would do all that was in my power to get well but the rest I would surrender over to life itself. I begged it to hear my desperate plea to live and use all its power to help me. A good week or so after my second diagnosis, my mind started to clear somewhat. Initially after the diagnosis, I had been screaming all sorts of profanities at the skies. How could life desert me and let me die when throughout my life I had been so conscious of and grateful for this powerful presence which connects us all? I was livid and terrified, but gradually I was beginning to see that cancer didn't have to be a death sentence for me. Despite what I was being told, I realised that I could have another shot at life and that this time I would experience things differently. I began to see that this really was the universe giving me one last chance. I didn't know what the outcome for me would be but I was beginning to feel that there might be a chance I would live for longer than I was expected to.

Then I had a severe anaphylactic reaction to my second dose of chemo. I felt my throat tightening very quickly and was soon unable to breathe. I pushed the alarm button and half an hour of chaos and panic ensued. The medical team were brilliant and I was conscious throughout. I had no pulse and I remember thinking that this was not how I was supposed to die, especially as I hadn't had a chance to say good bye to my family. Then I quickly calmed myself and focused on a mantra I repeated over and over again in my head – 'I am calm and all is well'. After an adrenalin shot was given to me, I remember my sense of relief as I heard the doctor's voice saying "she's going to be ok. The colour is returning to her face". He had been so calm throughout, holding my hand as he issued commands to the nurses and I will be eternally grateful for his comforting presence.

I started a new regime on a strong combination of drugs and continued that for six months. I had my first PET CT scan in July 2014, which showed a reduction of around 70% in metabolic activity. Then in October I started taking oral chemo, but continued with a drug, Avastin, through my portacath every three weeks. My next scan in October showed complete metabolic remission. It was in effect a normal scan. The oncologist was amazed. I was scanned a couple more times over the next eighteen months, each showing clear results, and continued with my regime although I was beginning to feel my body really needed a break from the toxicity.

Initially I had huge faith in my oncologist but he admitted to me that he was aggressive in his treatment and I was beginning to feel frustrated by my inability to be open and honest with him about my desire to stop drugs, and his constant fear-mongering. He never allowed me to be positive and hopeful but would always remind me how close to death I was. He was later to tell me that if I didn't take the drugs, I would be dead within six months. I wasn't. His tone was always negative and melodramatic, and this was beginning to annoy me, as I was convinced he was over dramatising things. I know he was well-meaning though – this was just how he dealt with things and there was no denying his incredible expertise when it came to conventional treatment.

I had responded so well to treatment but I knew that what I had been doing at home, in my own life, was the biggest contributor to this. I had been rushed into treatment but was reading and researching avidly and making huge changes to my life. I started ensuring my diet was the best it could be. I was juicing, eating a plant-based diet with some wholegrains, and plenty of essential fats. I had found a nutritionist who specialised in cancer and she helped me with my diet and supplements. I slowed down, relaxed more, went for long, gentle walks and started meditating. I was finally learning to take care of myself.

The day after my second diagnosis, we were all set to complete on a house we had found after five years of searching. It was an old cottage, set in a couple of acres and had been lived in for over forty years by an elderly couple. It was in real need of updating. The water was from a spring, and fed to the house through an old galvanised pipe which occasionally got blocked by a frog. There were rats in the attic and the poorly built extension had no heating in it. However, the location was lovely, down a woodland track with a beautiful view from the house (once you cut the bramble away), a gurgling stream and a real sense of peace throughout.

We asked to delay by a week while I was having more tests done, and to visit one final time to decide whether we should take on this project. The last thing we wanted was for my husband to be left with a half-finished project, a busy job and three children to care for. We visited and I knew instantly we should go ahead. The peace and serenity surrounding the place was incredible. I knew that I would be able to cope with the disruption of building because I would have no choice. I was NOT going to get stressed about it. This home and its beautiful, peaceful surroundings were going to help me get well. We moved a month later. I don't know how we did it – pack up one home, unpack another whilst I was in and out of hospital and my husband busy at work, but we did it. I know that somehow it helped me put my energy into creating a future that I was determined to be here for.

It had been so hard telling the children. At that time I wanted to be optimistic and hopeful, yet get them to understand that my life would be shortened. I didn't do it very well. I was too optimistic and almost dismissed it, when telling my middle daughter, who was thirteen, and my son, who was eleven. I didn't give them enough time to absorb it, and busied myself being too positive and hiding my mixed feelings around the subject. I had told my eldest daughter, who was fifteen, on a walk we went on after school one day. The others were away and she got it. She understood the implications and that walk was one of the pivotal moments of our relationship, which was having its ups and downs, as any relationship between a teenage daughter and mother does. It felt as though I was talking to a grown woman and a few days later I received a note from her. It read as follows;

> "Dear Mummy,
>
> I suppose this is to make up for not writing you a birthday card. I did write you a letter before, however since Tuesday I thought I better rewrite one.
>
> I'm not really sure what to say other than I think the absolute world of you and couldn't wish for a better mother. You are an amazing women (*sic*) and very aspiring to me. You really are the best mother in the world. I seriously can't think of a single thing I'd change about you. You have brought me up perfectly (not that I'm perfect) and I can't thank you enough for that.
>
> Talking of which, I know I will need help when it comes to bringing up my own children so you better damn well be there when it comes to it. Though, even if you aren't there physically I know you will be spiritually and you'll be there to guide me no matter what. Writing this feels so unreal, I feel as if I've made

this all up in my head. I'm sorry if this is a little overdramatic, and I'm sorry if it was rude to say that. (I do know that was bad English). But dearest Mummy, I love you to the moon and back 100s of billions of times, and what do they say? Stars can't shine without darkness. I love you Mummy and I'll stay strong for you.

I'm sorry, I've never been great at writing my emotions however I think you should remember this; (my favourite quote which keeps me going)

'It's not about waiting for the storm to pass. It's about learning to dance in the rain.'

I have plenty more quotes if you need any, however, unfortunately they aren't said by Ghandi or Jesus, more like depressed teenage girls, however that means they are pretty deep.

I respect you so much, I can't imagine what you're going through but you have so many people to support you. Don't forget to smile. You are beautiful. Even more so than that lady. You are incredible Mummy, I'm so proud to be your daughter".

It had been hard physically first time round with young children, but this time it was harder emotionally. I worried about what they were really feeling but knew that the balance between being hopeful and realistic was a difficult one. As time went on though, my hope grew and I ignored the reality, which we were constantly being reminded of. As I became more hopeful, so too did my family.

With the diagnosis, I knew the area I needed to get to grips with was my mental and emotional health so I started meditating to try and quieten my mind. This had a profound effect on me, bringing a real sense of calm and clarity. I began to search for a therapist to help me deal with my unhealthy thinking, which I knew had contributed to my illness. I soon found one who was to be an incredible support to me, until I knew that I myself had the answers I needed to get well and no longer needed her help.

I had a lovely, long summer in 2015 without treatment (not intentional but I had fallen off the clinic's radar) and had stopped taking Avastin in the autumn, which brought an end to the crippling, three day migraines I had been having. However, I was not really taking the oral chemotherapy regularly, both forgetting and not really wanting to. I eventually wrote to my oncologist in February 2016 to ask him please to understand that I really wanted to stop all treatment for a while. I got the O.K.

As soon as I stopped taking the pills for good, however, I began worrying. I began waking in the middle of the night panicking and would send myself back off to sleep with the reassurance that I would start taking the pills the next day. In the morning, though, I would feel convinced again that I needed to stop and give my body a break. I knew I either needed to start taking the medication again or, if not, I needed to be fully convinced that I was doing the right thing and not have these feelings of anxiety and self-doubt. I continued without taking them yet having big doubts about what I was doing. I was also getting more complacent about the changes I had made. I began rushing around more, getting stressed about things, drinking too much, eating less well and not exercising as much as I wanted. It was all bothering me and I was feeling frustrated and guilty, but told myself I would see how my next scan went, scheduled for the end of April 2016. I told myself that whether there were signs of cancer or not, I would get myself back on track, be more disciplined and start looking after myself properly again. I knew that I was letting things slip a bit and that this wasn't the way forward.

The scan showed a recurrence of cancer in a few places in my back and pelvis – some old and some new sites. I wasn't really surprised, yet felt both cross with myself and stupid. It took a few days for the confusion to clear. Why had it returned? Was it because I had stopped conventional medicine? Well yes, but I knew there was more to it than that. I read a paragraph in David Hamilton's book "How your mind can heal your body" a month or so later, in which he talks about placebos and medicine. In it he says "sometimes circumstances take over our lives – we get lazy, we think we'll be ok now that the condition is pretty much cleared up – and we don't complete the course. But nagging doubts about what we 'should' have done occasionally enter our minds. It is these thoughts that cause the relapses.'(1) That hit the nail on the head for me.

I knew I wasn't ready to stop treatment. I still had too much self-doubt and just wasn't ready to go it alone, even though I still badly wanted a break from these drugs and a serious detox of my body. I continued taking the pills even though I didn't want to and felt they were doing more damage than good. I know that what we believe is important and doing something we feel is detrimental to ourselves, can be exactly that. So about a month after taking the pills again, I stopped. The fear had gone…apart from the odd moment. Food, exercise, relaxation and a different way of thinking were to be my medicine. My Achilles heel was a couple of relationships I had with people that were causing me a lot of anguish at the time, despite the fact I loved them dearly. I knew I needed to find better ways of coping but for various reasons, I found this hard to do. I had to be really disciplined mentally. I started running more or taking myself for long walks when I was finding things hard. I meditated when I was feeling hurt or stressed (not just in the morning) and this really helped me through many difficult months. I couldn't allow myself to stay in a negative place for too long and knew the only way to snap myself out of it was by doing something different, something that was going to calm my mind and make me feel better, but I can't pretend it was easy.

At the same time, I was lying to my oncologist and to most of my friends and family about taking the medication. I realise now that my head and heart were in different places, and that I had created a real conflict within myself. I knew what I wanted to do and felt it was absolutely right but couldn't be completely open about this, and go ahead with living my life as I wanted to. I was convinced I could get well and was feeling really good most of the time, but my focus was constantly on cancer. I belonged to a couple of facebook support groups which were great, but every day there were messages with advice or people's own stories – both positive and sad. My world was immersed in cancer and my trips to the clinic every three weeks accentuated this. So when my November scan showed progression in my skeletal system, I decided to come clean and be open, not just with my oncologist but my family and friends. I was going to turn my attention away from illness and onto life and good health. I left the facebook groups, which were no longer helpful to me, and decided that I needed to stop obsessing about getting that good scan.

I have created wellness but also illness. I have yo-yoed between the two for years now, trying to grapple with my mind. For me, without doubt, this illness is a disease of the mind and linked to an identity crisis, and no drug is going to be able to cure that. Only I can and over 40 years of self-sabotage means that it is taking a little longer than I wanted. I am in no rush though. I know that I have reached a place of balance and good health now. Almost a year on from my last scan, there has been no progression. I am in no pain and I am often reminded that I should be in substantial pain. I am also very much alive, even though I should have died last Christmas according to my first oncologist (I have since found a more positive, open-minded one). It is so easy to be fixated on the end result, that we miss the point and forget that getting there is the important part. I have been guilty of this for so long now and I feel it has really slowed my recovery, but now I am focusing on my day to day life, which I am so enjoying. Not every day is shiny and perfect by any means but I know the healing process is well underway. This healing goes far beyond 'curing' cancer and has given me a whole new experience of life.

I am sure that this disease will disappear from my body when I have learnt all I need to from it or maybe it will stay there as a constant reminder of what life is about....being ourselves, learning, loving and enjoying as we go along. One thing I know for sure is that it won't regress or stay stable if I don't focus on joy and living life now. You can live a wonderful life even if your physical body is not disease-free.

However, I have to face up to the fact that there is also the possibility that the disease will progress to such an extent that I do die. Although I firmly believe this won't be the case, if it is, will I be one of the many deemed by our culture to have 'lost my battle with cancer'? I will have lost time with those I love so dearly and also the opportunity to do the things I still want to do, but I will have gained a new kind of health and wellbeing through this experience. Death is not a failure. I would always choose a shorter life with my present awareness than a longer life living as I did –at double speed, numb to my experiences and a slave to my destructive mind. Whatever happens, cancer has marked a beginning for me, not an end.

*'Nothing ever goes away until
it teaches us what we need to know'*
Pema Chodron (American buddhist and author)

BELIEVE THAT YOU CAN GET WELL

Cancer does not have to be a death sentence, even with a poor prognosis. There are patients the world over beating the odds all the time. They are living way beyond medical expectations either with or without conventional medicine Treatment is becoming more personalised and there are more options available to us. Certain patients and doctors are waking up to the realisation that when patients start to take responsibility for their own health and wellbeing, and stop being so dependent on doctors to get them well, real healing can occur. Of greatest significance is the part we ourselves play in our own health.

What is needed is a real willingness to tackle the different areas of our health that need tackling and this may mean making some real changes to our lives. We just need to learn about what good health really means. Our body has an incredible capacity to heal itself and what often prevents it from doing so is our own limited thinking as humans, the fear that surrounds cancer and an unwillingness to make healthy changes (or a lack of understanding about what changes to make). However, we can learn to support our body's healing ability by how we live and how we think. We are not powerless. In fact the opposite is true, and these challenging and seemingly hopeless times in our lives are actually the times when we are presented with the biggest opportunities to create what we want in our lives and implement profound change.

It is time to wake up, protect ourselves from the fear that is endemic in our culture and know that we can get well. Cancer is reversible and if we believe this with our whole heart, we can begin the healing process. We just need to start listening to and looking after ourselves – body, mind and spirit. If we are unable to heal our physical bodies in the long run, we can still heal ourselves emotionally and experience real wellbeing in the time we have left.

'Believe that you have it, and you have it'.
Latin proverb

FEEL THE FEAR...THEN MOVE ON

A cancer diagnosis is very scary, there is no denying that. We get pushed down the road of treatment very quickly and we can feel out of control and terrified. It is inevitable that you will experience this fear and indeed it is important that you do rather than suppress it, but don't let it overwhelm you. Fear is what grasps us, stuns us and stops us being proactive in our own healing, unable to see the bigger picture if we let it consume us. We have a very different approach to cancer here in the West than in other parts of the world, such as China and India, where it is essentially seen as an imbalance in one's mental, emotional and physical health. Anita Moorjani in her book 'Dying To Be Me' quotes her yoga and Ayurveda master as saying,

"Cancer is just a word that creates fear. Forget about the word and just focus on balancing the body. All illnesses are just symptoms of imbalance. No illness can remain when your entire system is in balance."(2)

It is natural to feel such fear when we pay so much attention to the statistics. Ignore them. They don't take into account anything that a person may be doing or experiencing in their personal lives. There are many people who get well and have no need for treatment and are not part of the statistics any longer and there are an increasing number of people who heal themselves with no treatment at all and are not part of the statistics either. When the cause of death is labelled as 'cancer', does it ever occur to us that sometimes it is the aggressive treatment and hopelessness that has maybe led to the death, not necessarily the disease itself.

We feel fear because we give cancer so much power. What if we, instead, put some trust in life, in ourselves and in our own bodies, which know what to do. We must help them by doing things to support them and focus more on what feels right and good. If we can start looking at it differently, at the bigger picture, then we can realise that rather than being a big problem, this is actually a big opportunity for profound growth and change. It is, so go with it and learn to support your body by being kinder and easier on yourself.

Do what FEELS right and you will start to find ways of moving on from the fear and hype surrounding cancer, and learn to replace it with determination and hope.

When you are immersed in fear, divert your attention to what you love and busy yourself with something you love doing. It takes a real awareness and determination to do so but it is possible and gets easier the more you do it. This is where I also found meditation to be crucial. It is a strong antidote to fear. Sitting quietly for only fifteen minutes daily has literally changed my life. I must have had one of the busiest and 'over-thinking' minds on the planet, but I have learnt how to access that place of inner calm and strength. By learning to find some stillness and peace in our daily lives, through meditation, relaxation or just learning to slow down, we can learn how to access our own inner strength, which will help us through periods of fear and doubt. Our own inner strength is formidable. Understand that fear is natural but it isn't helpful after a while, so move beyond it. Another incredible tool I discovered later, which would help with so many emotions but especially fear, was Emotional Freedom Technique (EFT). I discuss this later on in the book but many will have heard of this form of 'tapping' meridians in the body to release stuck emotions and pain. It really does work in my opinion.

We need to understand also that we can, ultimately, learn how to be masters of our own health. This may be scary for some, but I would say here, don't be daunted and don't rush into things. Getting well doesn't require you to know all the answers initially, but is a process, during which you may change direction or take different paths as you go along and learn, as with life in general. You don't have to know it all now. Just focus on what feels right for you and what you think your needs are right now, whilst you start to learn and educate yourself about how to improve your physical, mental, emotional and spiritual health.

'Courage is the power to let go of the familiar'
Raymond Lindquist (American Presbyterian pastor)

THERE IS NO UNIVERSAL WAY TO RECOVERY - THERE IS ONLY YOUR WAY

…and it will be different for every other patient. There is no single cure for cancer, but there are hundreds of different ways to support our body's healing. Cancer is a whole body disease, a multi-dimensional disease that will not give into one type of treatment. Add to that the fact that each cancer is different, and each patient is different, and it becomes clear that there cannot be a 'one size fits all' solution.

As I mentioned before, conventional treatment is becoming more personalised, which is good news, but we patients need to do our bit too and work out what that actually means. The way to do this is both to learn from other patients who have made significant changes and taken responsibility for their health and their lives, but also to take a long, hard look at ourselves and our lives, and be honest about what needs changing. We need to 'go within' and trust ourselves more to find our own path to recovery.

This is where we need the help of our INTUITION. We need to find ways of listening to 'it'…our gut feeling, through meditation and stillness. Finding your own way and being in the driving seat of your own recovery can also mean having to resist treatment or advice, which you are being offered or pressurised into taking by well-meaning friends or doctors. Be as relaxed and as open-minded as you can. Find some stillness and peace each day, so that you can think more clearly.

There is a mine of information out there on the more physical aspects of healing (different diets, vitamins and possible cures). It can be truly stressful trying to work it all out and make decisions, but if you can make time to relax and find that stillness every day, you will learn to access that intuition and trust it more each day. Remember also that there is a lot of support out there in terms of nutritionists, websites, books, psychologists and much more, and you will find the right help for yourself eventually, when you take the time to quieten your mind. Know too when to take a break from all the information you are being given or searching for. It is important to give yourself time to work out and pay attention to which decisions feel right for you. Take it one day at a time and try not to be overwhelmed. The more you relax physically and mentally, the more you will support your body to heal and your own impulses will guide you to what you need. This is a key area – resting and relaxing your body is vital to healing so make time to do it!

I never once asked the question 'why me' after either diagnosis. I knew the answer. I hadn't been looking after myself for years. I ate well, exercised, drank wine at weekends (and far too much at times) but my mental and emotional health was dire. I had been living a lie for years, denying my true self and my true path, and had lost my way and the will to live fully. I saw the world through black tinted glasses and wanted to fix the problems, but didn't know how to. Everywhere I looked, I saw a damaged and sick world, and though I desperately wanted to make it better, I didn't realise that focusing on these problems and feeling powerless to fix them, was bringing me down and making me ill. Unhealthy thinking put untold stress upon my body and the result was chronic illness.

So, alongside learning how to support my body by eating the right foods, exercising and learning to relax, I have made my mental and emotional health the key area of my recovery. This will not be the same for everyone, but it is an area which cannot be overlooked. Eating an anti- cancer diet is vital, but it is not enough if we have emotional issues that need dealing with, habitual negative thinking or an inability to deal with stress. I discuss these areas later in the book, and although changes won't occur overnight, learning to let go and gradually shift your thinking will have dramatic effects on your life and health.

Never compare what you are doing to anybody else. Everyone is at different stages in their health and their awareness. Be open to learning from them but you will know what you need if you just find the space and time to listen. Keep it simple – is what you are eating going to nourish your body, is how you are thinking helpful to you, are you resting and relaxing enough? You do know, deep down, what you need and what is supporting you and what is not.

'We are drowning in information, while starving for wisdom'
E.O. Wilson (American biologist, researcher and author)

FIND THE BALANCE

Cancer can have many causes, which all come down to STRESS. Stress can be physical, mental or emotional and they all weaken our immune systems. Therefore, when dealing with cancer, we need to tackle all areas of our health and bring ourselves into balance.

Cancer only really develops in an individual whose immune defences have been weakened. It cannot thrive where an immune system is strong and healthy. There are many factors which put stress on our immune systems – depression, junk food, chemicals in the environment, emotional stress and trauma to name but a few. If we can limit the amount of stress from such factors, if we can do everything we can to strengthen our systems, we can get and stay well. Good sleep, nutritional food, sex, laughter, exercise, relaxation, stroking our pets – they are all good for us. Doing more of what we love, eating nutritious wholefoods, relaxing and being happy will affect us far more positively than we realise.

Kelly Turner, a researcher and psychotherapist, was counselling cancer patients at a large hospital in San Francisco. Upon hearing about a case of radical remission in a book she had read, she set out to try and find other cases of radical remission. She defines radical remission as occurring when cancer disappears without the patient using conventional medicine at all, or when conventional medicine fails and the patient switches to alternative methods and the cancer disappears, or lastly when a patient uses both conventional and alternative methods to outlive a dire prognosis (i.e. where the five year survival rate is 25% or less). She couldn't understand why cases of radical remission were largely ignored rather than being closely studied.

Her extensive research into these cases and what these long-term survivors had done in order to get well resulted in her book "Radical Remission". Although she identified numerous factors that could potentially have played a role in radical remission, there were nine recurrent factors which the survivors all mentioned doing in order to get well. They were as follows;

Radically changing one's diet
Following one's intuition
Taking control of your health
Having strong reasons for living
Increasing one's positive emotions
Releasing suppressed emotions
Embracing social support
Using herbs and supplements
Deepening one's spiritual connection.

When I eventually read this book, I was struck by how many of these factors were not in fact physical factors but mental, emotional and spiritual ones, reinforcing my conviction that a strong body-mind-spirit system is essential to good health. It seems incredible that we have been 'fighting a war' against cancer for so long now and yet research into long-term survivors has been so absent in the world of medical research. Surely we have a lot to learn from them?

It is apparent then that a willingness to look at the different areas of our health that need addressing, including changing old ways of behaviour, is vital to our recovery alongside an understanding and belief that we ourselves do have the ability to get better. Having conventional medicine can buy us time while we sort out our lives and make the changes we need to. It can also debilitate us if we don't prepare for it and the mental, emotional and physical stress it can put us under. Either way, it will not heal our lives. Only we ourselves and our 'physicians within' can do that. We just need to educate ourselves about how to improve our mental, emotional, physical and spiritual health and then get on and make the changes we need to. Pay attention to what nature is telling you and cooperate with your body to get the healing process started. We can't just treat the symptoms of this illness, we must treat the cause, and we need to do so in a calm and relaxed manner as opposed to a desperate, anxious and fearful attempt to fix ourselves. Relax and focus on health not cancer.

'The part can never be well unless the whole is well'
Plato

IT DOESN'T HAVE TO BE A BATTLE

We have been waging war on cancer for years and it hasn't really worked.

We all have different ways of approaching things but waging war usually causes more damage and misery. I believe that like most upheavals in our lives, the suffering we experience is actually happening for us rather than to us. These difficult times in our lives, these things that nearly break us, are really the things that teach us so much and make us see things more clearly. They are the things that make us whole, so what is to be gained from fighting them? Listen to them, learn from them and maybe even be grateful for them. They are here to help you, even if you can't see it yet. There is no surprise that so many people feel that cancer was the best thing that ever happened to them. It can teach us to rethink things, to go within and get in touch with our innermost selves. It offers us an experience which I believe is primarily about reconnecting with who we are. We can lose sight of that in our frenetic, crazy lives. We can lose sight of who and what matters to us. We can lose sight of what our needs are and how to tend to them, and of the fact that life is so much richer when we learn to 'go with the flow', but also understand that we can create the changes we want to.

The well-known Serenity prayer reads,

> 'God grant me the serenity to accept the things I cannot change, courage to change the things I can, and wisdom to know the difference'.

Cancer has answered this prayer for me, teaching me to be more aware of my thinking and the way I eat and live yet able to let go of control of many other things, surrendering to the flow of life.

When you are feeling so physically ill or mentally exhausted from this illness, try to just go with it rather than fight it, and know that it will pass. I remember that whenever I have been in great pain, either from this illness or as a migraine sufferer, I have felt myself resisting or fighting the pain. It never works. When I have breathed through the pain, and just accepted it is there, I have been more relaxed and it has really eased the intensity of it. It may seem irritating to be told to 'breathe through' or 'go with' pain, but it is much more effective than resisting or fighting it. I no longer get migraines after years of suffering. I decided that I was living in fear of the next one, wondering when it would come, and that I needed to accept that I could handle them - that if I felt one coming, I would just relax and tell myself that I would be fine. I had spent years desperately searching for ways to stop them. When you are struggling, tell yourself that things will get better and that your body knows what to do. Relax, breathe and let it do its job. Be kind and gentle on yourself and things will change.

Get out of your head and learn to 'feel' what feels right more. If things are tough, just try to do or think of things that make you feel better, and this will shift things. Use your imagination when your current reality doesn't feel good. You are helping your body and mind relax and feel better, and doing more good than you can possibly imagine.

"Whatever you fight, you strengthen, and what you resist, persists."
Eckhart Tolle (German-born spiritual teacher and author)

LET FOOD BE THY MEDICINE

There is so much advice and information on the right anti-cancer diet out there, with information changing and new research all the time. It can be overwhelming. What you eat matters enormously and is a key way to support your body to heal. Evidence is overwhelming that radically changing our diet can make all the difference to our recovery and many cancer patients will say it has been the single most contributory factor to their recovery. It is the easiest way to impact your physical, mental and emotional health quickly. Not just cancer but many conditions can be overcome when we change our diet and there is now an abundance of stories about people who have changed difficult health conditions through their diet. There is no question that you will feel so much better when you start eating healthy and nourishing foods.

We need to be informed but we also just need some common sense amidst the overload of information out there. Vegetables are good for you and the most important part of a good diet. Sugar is not and cancer loves it. Eating organic is way better than eating sprayed food but if your budget really won't allow it, eat many more vegetables anyway. There are so many weird and wonderful ingredients, let alone more common ones with amazing nutritional benefits and anti-cancer properties. Don't worry about which ones to take and rush into spending loads of money on them. You will discover and learn as you go along and adjust your diet according to what you feel is best and what stage of your recovery you are at. Eating a well balanced, anti-cancer diet does not need to be expensive at all.

At the back of the book I have included some charts and further information on the right foods but I will list the basics here, which I have taken from David Servan-Schreiber, Kris Carr and Michele Wolff's books, alongside my more recent time at the Living Foods Institute in Atlanta, U.S. Try and get some expert advice from a nutritionist or naturopath but remember to listen to your body as well. I really feel that changing your diet to a well-balanced vegan diet, with the majority of food being raw, is the best thing you can do initially. When things are more calm and under control, then you can start adding good quality fish or meat alongside other foods.

What you put in to your body is either going to help healing or not, but don't get so fanatical about it, that it causes you stress. That is defeating the point. I have had times when I have been away or on holiday and not been able to eat a great anti-cancer diet. Getting stressed about it is worse than the fact I was eating a non-perfect diet. It was much more important that I enjoy the time wherever I was and whoever I was with. If you are away from home, you can either do the best you can or it really isn't hard to take foods with you that you have prepared earlier or ingredients to make the meals you want to eat.

Be level-headed and use your common sense. Of course it makes sense to do as much as you can to support your body as it gets on with its job of healing, so educate yourself about how best to do this, but also do what feels right. I realise that feeling in control of our food and diet can help us feel better about managing our health, but letting go a bit (and I don't mean going crazy here), and making it more enjoyable is important too. This is a big part of our lives so make it work for you and your body, and remember that you will want to adjust your eating habits according to what you are learning and the state of your health at different times. Here are the basics to remember;

1. Eat loads of vegetables, and remember that green vegetables are best.

2. The more raw and organic, the better so try and make as much of your diet as possible consist of raw food (fruits, vegetables, seeds, nuts and unprocessed oils). Cooking food above 118 degrees kills the enzymes but if you are cooking food, don't overcook it and learn to cook slowly. Steam or stir fry. Only cook with oils which remain stable under high heat, such as coconut oil, rice bran oil and animal fats (if you are not on a strict vegan diet) such as ghee, butter and lard.

3. Get sprouting. You can sprout lentils, chickpeas, mung beans etc – it is cheap and easy to do and they are one of the most alkaline, nourishing and oxygenating foods we can eat - even better than raw, since they are still 'living'. Look into the work of Ann Wigmore, which is what I learnt about at the Living Foods institute in Atlanta and which has helped many people heal from serious diseases.

4. Cut out sugar. Cancer LOVES it. Use natural substitutes if you need to sweeten your food, such as stevia, yucon syrup, agave, xylitol, raw honey and maple syrup but try to use very sparingly. I have heard that stevia is the best as it is low-glycemic but check ingredients as some products only contain 1% stevia. Fruit does contain sugar but also loads of nutritional benefits. All fruit is ok in moderation (unless you are on a ketogenic diet) but the best ones are berries, citrus (lemons, limes and grapefruit) and stone fruit (especially plums). Again, some people would say no to any fruit because of its sugar content, whereas others (such as Chris Wark) strongly disagree.

5. Cut out the bad carbs and don't overdo the good ones. Essentially, all carbs break down into glucose. Complex carbs are the good ones such as wholegrains and pulses, but they can be hard to digest so I soak them overnight before I use them. Simple or refined carbs are the bad guys and they include potatoes, bread, pasta, cheese crackers etc. Cut out anything that comes from white flour.

6. Cut down or eliminate dairy, meat and fish. We are eating way too many animal products and although good quality pasture fed meat and wild fish do have benefits, we don't need much of it. Red meat causes inflammation and is acidic. Processed meat has finally been recognised as being carcinogenic and animal fat, in general, has been linked to cancer. There is also so much research showing direct links between dairy consumption and cancer, along with many other ailments such as Crohn's disease, eczema, asthma and

arthritis. (3) As Kris Carr reminds us in her book, we can get all the protein and calcium we need from a well-balanced plant-based diet, so going vegan is really a good idea if you have cancer.

7. Avoid hydrogenated fats (transfats) and foods which contain them as they are very bad for you. Examples are margarine, biscuits, dips, snacks, canola oil and peanut butter. Instead, ensure you are getting the right oils into your body from sources such as coconut oil, olive oil, olives, nuts, seeds, macadamia and apricot kernel oil. Coconut oil has a number of benefits. Also ensure you are eating plenty of oils rich in Omega 3 (flaxseed oil, chia seeds, hempseed oil, UDO's oil).

8. Eat plenty of anti-inflammatory foods as inflammation has been linked to many chronic diseases, especially cancer. Omega 3 fatty acids (as discussed above) are a really important part of such a diet and most Western diets are severely lacking in them. Fish oil (best from Krill) is a rich source of this and something I take daily. You can sprinkle chia seeds on everything and I grind flaxseeds up and add to my smoothie (best kept whole in a freezer). Chia seeds are easier to digest if soaked first but it isn't necessary.

Ginger, hot red peppers, garlic and green tea are all great. The king of the anti-inflammatory foods though is TUMERIC. Its anti-cancer benefits are quite astounding, especially when it is cooked with oil and used with ground black pepper and/or ginger. Start making lots of curries. I include it daily and heat up some almond milk with half a teaspoon of cinnamon, a teaspoon of tumeric and some black pepper. It's delicious. Alternatively, I add some whole turmeric, when I can get hold of it, or some powdered turmeric to a smoothie. Just mix it in a nutribullet or vitamix with some ground black pepper, almond milk, berries, kale or other greens. Remember to get hold of good quality turmeric though, such as Organic

Traditions concentrated powder, a quarter of a teaspoon of which equates to 88g of fresh turmeric.

9. I would really suggest you invest in a juicer or a means to make smoothies. They are such an easy and quick way of getting loads of greens into your body and of course put little strain on your digestive system, which is so vital to health. They help reduce inflammation, and give you your daily shot of vitamins, minerals, enzymes and proteins without you having to eat heaped plateful after plateful of vegetables. Green is best as it won't cause your blood sugar levels to rise as much as starchier vegetables like carrot and beetroot. I add ginger, garlic and parsley or mint. Smoothies mean you get more fibre than a juice but are more effort for your body to digest. Both are great though I believe you are getting more nutrition and energy from a smoothie. You can add nutritional powders to either, such as chlorella, spirulina or wheatgrass. I grow my own wheatgrass, which is very simple to do. You can get the seeds, along with sunflower, pea sprouts and numerous others from www.aconbury.co.uk. This company offer a lot of support and advice.

10. Add plenty of herbs and spices to your food – they all have great benefits.

11. If you do the above you will be eating a predominantly alkaline diet which is what you want to be doing. The more alkaline our bodies are, the more oxygen they have. Cancer hates oxygen and thrives in an acidic environment. Our tissues and blood need to be slightly alkaline for optimum health, and most ailments can be traced back to acidity inside our bodies.(4) It is much easier for our bodies to be acidic rather than alkaline, as they are constantly dealing with naturally occurring acids that are the by-product of respiration, metabolism and exercise. Then we are constantly topping up levels with our acidic diet and lifestyles. Poor diet, anger, stress and lack of

exercise all create acidity in our bodies. See the back of the book for a list of top acidic/alkaline books but remember the simplest way to alkalise our bodies is to eat a plant-based diet with an emphasis on raw and living foods. Breathing deeply alkalises the blood too so learn to be aware of and change your breathing. Cut out sugar, start drinking water with lemon squeezed into it (very alkalising but plays havoc with your teeth so drink through a straw) and eat loads of green vegetables. Michele Wolff recommends eating one umeboshi plum a day too. They are salted Asian plums, which you can find in most health shops, and are very alkalising.

12. It is really important to do as much as we can to help our digestive system by eating the right foods which are easy to digest and also by detoxing. I discuss this in the next chapter but we will heal faster if we divert energy from digesting our food (which uses huge amounts of energy) to healing our bodies. Soak all nuts and seeds for at least 2 hours before eating them, or overnight.

Food is such a big part of our lives. The healthier you eat, the more you will crave healthy food and enjoy it. Get more informed and in the meantime, use your common sense and don't let yourself be overwhelmed. The most important thing needed to be successful in changing one's diet and helping our bodies heal, is the right mindset. If we embark on the task of changing our diets with a sense of dread and foreboding, then our experience will be miserable (speaking from my own experience at times).

However, if we look at it from the view point that we are helping support our bodies to heal and that some changes will be life-long changes, which will benefit us physically, mentally and emotionally and others can be relaxed once we get to a better place in our physical health, then the whole experience will be so much easier and more enjoyable.

Just go for it and make good choices but don't beat yourself up about things too much either. The guilt and judgement we impose on ourselves is far more detrimental than the failed attempts to be 'perfect'. Do the best you can and keep your focus on putting nourishing and beneficial foods into your body. Be positive.

DETOXIFICATION AND TAKING CARE OF YOUR GUT

In my research on diet, I have only more recently discovered the importance of the digestive system, and the fact that a healthy gut makes a healthy person. About 70% of the immune system is located in the gut, as this is the area which has to deal with eliminating toxins. So we need to really look after our gut and eating an anti-cancer diet is going to go a long way in accomplishing this. However, we can do more.

One really important way in which we can keep our digestion system healthy is to detox. Detoxing is the process of eliminating toxins that are in our bodies. Our bodies are just not designed to cope with the amount of toxins that are now part of our lives, so it is essential we not only try and limit them but also set aside times to cleanse our bodies of these toxins. Most toxins come from a poor diet, from drugs (medical and recreational), from the environment (such as car fumes and pesticides), from chemicals and electromagnetic radiation in our homes. Toxins are also produced within our bodies by stress, unfriendly bacteria in the gut and yeasts or parasites living in the digestive system. Cleansing our body and then helping restore and revive our health through good nutrition is really essential for us all but especially those of us who are ill. It is a process that involves the liver, kidneys, intestines, lungs, skin, blood and lymphatic circulatory systems.

Modern life is putting a big strain on our energy reserves, but one of the biggest drains on our systems is the digestion of food and this is even more of an issue when what we consume is of little nutritional value. The natural process of detoxification gets put on hold while the body digests our food but we can help restore the process by putting digestion on hold frequently and for long enough. If we can have our evening meal at a time that ensures we will have at least twelve hours until breakfast, that will allow for detoxification and healing during the night. According to Alejandro Junger in his book 'Clean', the detox signal is given about eight hours after your final meal of the day. The process of detoxification itself needs at least four hours to function properly. The larger the meal, the longer it takes to digest. If we can substitute meals with liquid meals then the food is almost ready for absorption and doesn't need to be broken down. If your breakfast is a smoothie, for example, or your evening meal a soup, this is going to really help (or better still if both meals are liquid). Even just cutting down on the size of your evening meal and having a twelve hour gap until breakfast is a really good way of supporting your body. A three day water fast or green juice fast is really manageable and there is now significant research into the benefits of fasting. It is such a simple way of diverting the body's energy away from digestion to healing. Of course, if you are ill and losing weight then you need to ensure you are putting enough fuel in your body through a balanced diet with plenty of healthy fats.

Enzymes are needed for digestion so if we eat cooked foods, the body has to manufacture them which uses up a lot of energy. Raw foods already contain the enzymes which are necessary for their own digestion. Avoiding foods which are difficult to digest and are known to cause food allergies (such as dairy, eggs, gluten, peanuts and sugar) will aid detoxification further. Fermented foods contain friendly bacteria which are so important for good gut health. They are extremely rich in enzymes, pre-digested protein and lactobacillus bacteria. I include two really easy recipes at the back of the book for a fermented drink (Rejuvelac) and a fermented food called Vegekraut, which is basically a type of sauerkraut.

Exercise is another important way to detox as we sweat through our skin, our largest organ. We really need to make sure we are working up a sweat a few times a week at least. Wearing deodorant is not helpful at all so use a natural one if you need to use it. Skin brushing before a shower is a really good way to detox (always brush up towards the heart), as is adding Epsom salts or Himalayan salt to a bath. I start each day with a glass of water and lemon juice, which cleanses the lymphatics and helps the liver function properly. Coffee enemas are really easy to do at home and are cheap and very effective. In fact, cleansing the colon either through colonic hydrotherapy with a trained therapist or by doing water or coffee enemas at home, is an important and highly effective way of eliminating built-up toxic waste in the colon.

A good detox will reduce blood acidity and levels of inflammation, stress and toxicity in our bodies, thus improving the environment in our cells which determine gene expression. If we have inherited 'bad genes', we now know that they can be turned on or off – 'expressed' or 'not expressed'. Gene expression can be influenced by our thoughts, emotions, the food we eat and the toxicity levels in our bodies. Healthy lifestyle choices have a direct impact but the impact of food on the way our genes are expressed is probably the greatest of these and is called 'nutrigenomics'. Eating the right foods and detoxing now and then is a vital way to turning off genes, which we might have inherited and predispose us to illness.

The digestive system really is vital to our health and deserves much attention, so try and make sure you are supporting it as best you can.

Here are the main points to remember to help support your digestive system, and they ARE important: drink water frequently and in between meals rather than with them (before is best), eat slowly and really chew your food really well, eat without distractions and in peace, eat evening meals before 7pm, eat healthy snacks if you are hungry rather than letting blood sugar levels dip, have colonics if you can afford them and/or learn about water/coffee enemas to do at home, try and have some meals as liquid meals and do a juice or water fast now and then.

VITAMINS, MINERALS AND SUPPLEMENTS

This is a huge area and an important one if you are trying to recover from a chronic illness such as cancer. Intensive farming means that the food we are now eating contains a fraction of the nutrients it did decades ago. We need to increase our intake of the right nutrients and each of us has different needs. I did some research initially and eventually found a nutritionist who had an expertise in cancer (see resources). She was extremely good and she really got me going with the right kind of diet and supplements, which need to be of good quality.

More recently, though, I have used the Quantum Biofeedback programme, which was originally developed by Professor William C Nelson, whilst working on the Apollo 13 project. It is the result of 20 years of research and is constantly being updated. This incredible test can detect energetic imbalances of vitamin levels, nutrients, minerals, enzymes, hormonal levels, disease, toxins, viruses and much more in our bodies. It can reveal where problems are and then alter the energetic imbalances. It was able to test which of the supplements I was on were actually beneficial to me and which were of no use, and to recommend others that were needed. It does a whole lot more and I have added the information and website in the resources section.

I would seriously advise you to seek professional help in this area, as it can be overwhelming and easy to waste money, but if you really cannot afford the advice of a nutritionist, naturopath or integrative medicine doctor, then the following are some key points to remember.

There is no point taking loads of vitamin supplements if you aren't getting enough minerals from your diet. To ensure you are, eat lots of vegetables, especially green, leafy ones, seaweeds and vegetable juices. Stress, pollution, acidic diets all contribute to reducing the level of minerals in our bodies. A liquid trace minerals supplement is a great choice. Two-time Nobel Prize winner Linus Pauling said "You can trace every sickness, every disease, every ailment to mineral deficiency." (5) I take "UltraTrace" by the brand Higher Nature. Alternatively, or additionally, take a good multivitamin and mineral supplement, and if you are eating vegetarian/vegan diet, ensure it has vitamin B12 in it.

There is a vitamin D deficiency epidemic at the moment and this is said to play a role in almost every major disease including cancer. Few foods naturally contain vitamin D so our main source is from the sun. It is vital for strong bones and a strong immune system. However, it is important to get the right amount for you and that will vary enormously on how heavy you are, how much body fat you have, where you live, what time of year it is and how often you get outside etc. Frank Lipman, doctor and author of 'Revive; Stop Feeling Spent and Start Living Again' recommends getting your vitamin D blood levels tested. If it is above 45ng/ml he recommends taking 2,000-4,000 IU a day. If, however, your level is 30-45ng/ml, he suggests starting with 5,000 IU a day for 3 months and then rechecking. If levels are less than 30ng/ml, he suggests starting with 10,000 IU a day and checking again after 3 months. 2,000-4,000 IU a day would be the maintenance dose.(6) Having said that I have been advised to take a high dose of 20,000iu for 3 months only. Get your bloods tested for their vitamin D levels and get the right advice.

A good probiotic is essential for health and especially digestive function. Probiotics help suppress harmful bacteria, improve immune function, enhance the protective barrier of the digestive tract and help produce vitamin K, a deficiency which is now being linked to cancer. Make sure you take one which is high in lactobacillus and bifidobacterium. I take "acidophilus – bifidus complex" by Vega. Stay away from antibiotics if you can, but if you have to use them, make sure you use a good probiotic afterwards, to restore the balance of good bacteria in your gut, which will have been destroyed alongside the bad bacteria.

More recently I have heard more and more about the link between an iodine deficiency and cancer (and other diseases such as heart disease and depression) though there is some controversy about taking high levels of it. I was advised to take a drop of Lugol's solution each day. You can buy it on Amazon. I also add dulse (seaweed) flakes to a lot of my food and salad dressings.

Organic Amla powder (Indian gooseberry) contains the highest known level of vitamin C in the plant kingdom – 20 times more than that of an orange. It has been used in Ayurvedic medicine for years and also enhances food absorption, balances stomach acid, regulates the elimination of free radicals and acts as an antioxidant. You only need quarter to half a teaspoon daily mixed in a little water. It is very bitter and doesn't taste good but is cheap and easy to source and well worth making part of your daily routine.

Remember that an organic, well-balanced, alkaline diet is going to give you a lot of the vitamins and minerals you require, especially if you are eating a high quantity of raw food, so get your diet in tip-top shape before you start spending lots of money on supplements.

GET MOVING

We all know that exercise releases endorphins and energises us, making us feel good and strengthening our immune systems. However, there are other effects it has on our bodies. It also lessens the amount of fat tissue we have in our bodies, which is where carcinogenic toxins are stored. It helps restore our hormonal balance, reducing excess oestrogen and testosterone within our bodies. It helps reduce inflammation and it fills our body with oxygen, cancer's big enemy. It provides the pump needed to move lymph around your body, which is essential for carrying oxygen to the tissues and removing waste material from them. It boosts T-cell production, which is vital in helping our immune system to function in general and especially in tackling cancer. It is also the best way to help weak bones and prevent osteoporosis – way more effective than any calcium supplements. Remember too that it is one of the best ways to help our bodies detox.

I am naturally a fairly active person but, like many, need motivating to exercise regularly. I used to go to a weekly yoga class and then try and go for a run twice or three times a week, on top of my daily dog walk. It was hard, therefore, to have such severe bone pain that it hurt to walk, let alone run. Even yoga became impossible until I had radiotherapy. I had to push away the feelings of frustration and guilt that came with not being able to move properly, and learn to relax more. I took up swimming and Tai chi instead, and then gradually, as things got better, I began to push myself to walk faster and further. I am now running again and loving it. Although I used to procrastinate and find any excuse not to go, I now know that the feelings of mental wellbeing I get after a run are worth the effort. I also practice yoga, going to a weekly class and try to do some stretches every day. I have found yoga to be vital to my recovery and would recommend it to everyone. There are so many free online yoga classes you can do. It tones, detoxifies, stretches aching muscles and limbs, relaxes, energises and most importantly helps us to focus on our breathing. When we practice yoga, we are breathing properly, supplying our organs with the oxygen vital for our health and helping eliminate toxins from our bodies. Do not underestimate the importance of deep breathing. I make a habit of breathing slowly and deeply when I am driving or in traffic – multi-tasking.

I know that it is just not worth neglecting regular exercise. If I do, I end up feeling frustrated, guilty and tired. It is a matter of finding what you enjoy doing, what works for you and making the effort to push yourself a bit. There is overwhelming evidence now that exercise is a vital part of recovery from disease and our health in general, and it doesn't have to cost anything. It is so much better to exercise and eat well than spend money on endless supplements, lotions and potions. We just need to make movement a part of our everyday lives, tapping into the energy of life. Move more, be less sedentary and find some forms of exercise you enjoy. Being more active means getting out there, living and enjoying life more – it can only make you feel better, physically and mentally, so find what works for you. And one more thing – get outside. Surround yourself in nature – it soothes the mind and soul and is one of the most uplifting remedies out there. I haven't perhaps placed enough importance on this as for me, being outside, whether exercising, walking or gardening has always been a vital component of my life. I would recommend spending time outdoors in nature as an essential part of anyone's recovery. Nature heals – there is no question about that in my mind.

WHAT CAN WE DO ABOUT ENVIRONMENTAL TOXINS?

It doesn't make happy reading learning about pollutants – chemicals released into the environment which are dangerous to our health. They are in pesticides, carpets, cosmetics, cleaning products, exhaust fumes, plastics, electromagnetic radiation, paint, furniture, x-rays, fly spray…the list goes on.

However, there is plenty we can do. We can buy environmentally friendly products to clean with (or use vinegar, bicarbonate of soda and lemon juice). We can get healthy choices of cosmetics and skincare from health shops and online. It really is important not to use chemicals on our skin. They can be more expensive but shop around and you will find reasonably priced ones or you can make your own if you want. I have a friend who does and I often mix essential oils with coconut oil as a hand or face cream. Just make sure you use organic 100% pure essential oil. Essential oils are powerful and have real healing properties. Inhale them or rub a drop in your hands and put over your ears or the soles of your feet, both of which have all the corresponding parts of the body mapped out on them.

Have your windows open as much as possible and get rid of your microwave (very high emitter of EMFs). Put a cactus near your computer which, like a Himalayan salt lamp, is supposed to absorb radiation. There are various products we can buy to put on our phones, computers and other devices to help dissipate EMFs and turn your WIFI off when you aren't using it. We can buy plastic containers and water bottles that are BPA free and use safe pots and pans to cook with (stainless steel, glass and ceramic as opposed to aluminium or teflon coated).

Ourselves and our families will all benefit, and so gradually will the world if more of us make these switches. I have to be honest that I now try and find a balance between being educated about the dangers of these pollutants and not allowing myself to be overwhelmed and depressed by too much information. It is all a matter of doing what you can, making better choices and using more natural products.

MEDITATE

Whatever your feelings are about meditation, I highly recommend you make it a daily practice. I know that my commitment to meditate each morning for only fifteen minutes or so has been instrumental in my recovery. I have spent my life searching outside of myself for all the answers, hoping to find them in books, medicine, religion and so on but have since learnt to find that place within me that has all those answers. I have learnt how to listen and tune into that part of me that I would call the soul. It is the part where we find our intuition, our gut feelings, our wisdom and deep inner peace. As Eckhart Tolle said "true intelligence operates silently. Stillness is where creativity and solutions to problems are found."

When we quieten our minds and connect spiritually, positive changes occur in our bodies, such as improved digestion and detoxification, decreased blood pressure, a reduction in levels of harmful hormones in the body and a strengthening of the immune system.(7) During relaxation and meditation, our resistance to disease and our body's ability to fight cancer is really strengthened. In fact, as Deepak Chopra mentions in his book 'The Ultimate Happiness Prescription', meditation activates our brains to release neurotransmitters, all of which are linked to happiness. These neurotransmitters include dopamine (an antidepressant), serotonin (linked to self-esteem), oxytocin (a pleasure hormone) and opiates (the body's own painkillers).

There is now ample research showing that meditation has significant, beneficial effects on our health and wellbeing. One study in Wisconsin showed that when a group of executives practiced mindful meditation for just eight weeks, significant changes were recorded to have taken place in the parts of their brain associated with optimism and positive mood. This was of course compared to a control group and to their previous states. Not only did they feel better but their immune systems were able to cope far better with the flu vaccine than those of the control group. (8)

A study with breast and prostate-cancer patients, doing the same programme, showed real benefit to their immune systems, with regard to both white blood cell and NK (natural killer) cell activity. They also reported sleeping better and feeling far more relaxed and content.(9)

Ian Gawler tells the story of his recovery from a particularly severe case of cancer in his book "You can conquer cancer." He was only given a few weeks to live by his oncologist after both amputation of his leg and a year of conventional treatments were unable to stop tumour growth. So, he began an intensive meditation practice and, quite quickly, he started getting better. After several months his bone deformities, which had been all over his chest, had completely gone. He is still alive today and has devoted the last thirty years to teaching about the benefits of meditation and healthy lifestyles, and the paramount importance of finding inner calm in our lives.

Some people may find it easier to do a guided meditation and there are just so many out there. You can download the 'Calm' app or use 'Hay House Meditations' or 'Meditation Oasis' and get their podcasts. I have always found that just closing my eyes, and focusing on my breath coming in through the top of my head as I inhale, and flowing through and out of my body as I exhale, is the most effective way of accessing this peace. As I inhale, I mentally say the word 'peace' and, as I exhale, 'release'. Some days my mind is way busier than other days and I find myself having to redirect my mind to the breath a lot. However, the sense of peace and calmness I get is incredible. By concentrating the mind and focusing the breath, I manage to connect with myself, to go 'within' and I begin to feel incredibly focused, strong and calm. It is a feeling that I can reach quickly at other times in the day or when things are difficult. I have my favourite meditations on my phone, which I can listen to while waiting for appointments, travelling or out and about.

However, meditation does more than just calm the mind and strengthen our resistance to disease. It brings us back to ourselves and to the flow of life which runs through us. When we reconnect with that flow of life, we can see the bigger picture – that whatever is happening to us in our lives is part of the natural order of things, and that ultimately we are connected to that flow of life. Disease happens when the mind/body/spirit connection is lost, so the more we connect to it, the more we open ourselves to healing.

We cannot afford to ignore our busy minds. The pace of our lives is becoming increasingly frenetic, and most of us are stressed out and many of us are ill. If we can learn to access our inner intelligence, we can begin to understand that we can learn from these challenges and difficulties and that they are there to help us move beyond where we are at the moment and break free from whatever is holding us back. More often than not it is fear (of something) that is holding us back and meditation is the way to access that formidable inner strength which we all possess. When we are fearless, there is nothing holding us back and no limitations as to what is possible. People say that meditation has changed their lives and I would agree with them. Setting aside ten or fifteen minutes of your day in exchange for real changes to your health and wellbeing is worth a try, don't you think?

'Inner silence promotes clarity of mind; it makes us value the inner world, it trains us to go inside to the source of peace and inspiration when we are faced with problems and challenges'
Deepak Chopra (American doctor, author and advocate of alternative medicine)

BE YOURSELF

There has been a fair amount of research into the 'cancer personality'. If you search online for 'cancer personality traits' numerous websites will tell you that having this type of personality weakens your immune system, and is described as being the sort of person who is passive, always trying to please others, suppresses their emotions, worries excessively and takes on too much. I was reminded of myself when I discovered this research.

Although there has been some controversy over this concept, what does seem to be more acceptable as an important factor in contributing to cancer is the feeling of helplessness. Bernie Siegel in his book "Love, Medicine and Miracles" talks about a gradual dissatisfaction with the role of housewife, which can lead to cancer in women if they do not find that role fulfilling. According to his research, housewives get fifty-four percent more cancer than the general population and one hundred and fifty-seven percent more than women who work away from home.(10) It is not the role itself that is dangerous but the unexpressed resentment that arises from this sacrifice. I find this research astonishing and it sends a clear message that we need to be a little more selfish and ensure that we are meeting some of our own needs.

Everything is relative and my life was not one I could complain about but I did. I felt overwhelmed by having three young children, the constant feeding, ironing and cleaning. Trying to be a good mother is exhausting. More importantly though, I had a mind that was wanting to fix the problems I saw around me but just couldn't see a way of doing so. Rather than pay attention to my emotions and do something about them, I would push them away and pretend that everything was alright, while my self-esteem was plummeting. I needed to calm my mind and to find some professional help to sort out my muddled thinking. I just couldn't see clearly.

It is only through this recent experience of illness that I have learnt how vital it is to be ourselves and make the changes we need to start living the life we want to live. There is nothing like a taste of one's own mortality to give you the confidence to be yourself at last. We have nothing to lose and everything to gain by doing so. Find a way of reconnecting with who you are and be that person. Ultimately only we can do this but we may need help getting there, in which case get it. There are so many therapies out there to choose from, such as cognitive behavioural therapy (CBT), neuro-linguistic therapy (NLP) or emotional freedom technique (EFT), which I discuss later.

It wasn't long ago that I read about the "Twelve steps to self-care" from the Happiness Institute, founded by Dr Tim Sharp, an internationally renowned leader in the field of positive psychology. These steps are reminders of how to be true to ourselves. They are as follows:

1. If it feels wrong, don't do it.
2. Say exactly what you mean.
3. Don't be a people pleaser.
4. Trust your instincts.
5. Never speak badly about yourself.
6. Never give up on your dreams.
7. Don't be afraid to say yes.
8. Don't be afraid to say no.
9. Be kind to yourself.
10. Let go of what you can't change.
11. Stay away from drama control and negativity.
12. LOVE.

They seem so obvious, yet many of us forget the importance of using them in our day to day lives. So find the courage to at last be yourself and not worry about what others think. The truth is other people aren't thinking, talking or focusing on us as much as we think. People are busy with their own lives. Really listen to what feels right for you, rather than what you or others think you ought to do and stop over-thinking things. Trying to be perfect and always do the right thing is tedious and joyless. Slow down and follow your heart more. Focus on who and what you love because the true self is always motivated by love. When you are being your true self, you are being the best of yourself and that part of yourself is fearless and loving. Love is stronger than fear. If you are feeling alone and unloved, then make loving yourself your focus.

"Like the moon, come out from behind the clouds. Shine!"
Buddha

BELIEVE IN YOURSELF

We all have a gut feeling about things, we all have intuition, but many of us have forgotten to listen to it. Meditation can help us find the stillness to listen to our intuition, but it doesn't have to be through meditation. It may be through listening to music, spending time in nature, gardening- anything or anywhere we can find some stillness. Being creative is really important, so take up a new hobby or rekindle an old one. As we listen to our inner wisdom, we start to do what is right for us and understand what our needs are. It does require us to 'go within' and listen, but as we do so and respond accordingly, we begin to gain confidence and believe in ourselves more.

As I started to look more closely at my life and gain more self-awareness, I realised that my life, and therefore my health, was so linked to how I felt about myself and that so many of my problems stemmed from low self-esteem. I had been suffering from low self-esteem to such an extent that I felt hopeless. I knew I needed to change my thinking and sought the help of a cognitive behavioural therapist to do so. It has taken commitment and time, but becoming aware of and stopping unhelpful and negative thinking has changed my life completely. I have learnt to stop constantly judging and criticising myself and instead to nurture, love and support myself more. It seems that when we start to take care of ourselves more, we gain confidence and self-esteem – that is what I have found. I have gradually learnt to believe in myself and when we believe in ourselves, anything is possible.

So, start believing in yourself. You know what's best for you and you know the answers. We are taught to listen to those in authority in our lives, such as teachers, parents and doctors, and so we forget to make our own decisions based on our inner knowing. It is just a matter of learning what your beliefs and values are and listening. It is your body and your life. Your experience of this illness may well be similar to others in the same situation, but it will also be different.

Make sure you surround yourself with the right support, and know that you do have the power to change things.

Have more faith in your body too. It is an incredible machine that really knows how to heal and what to do. It does require your help though. Relax, breathe, support it in the best ways you can and trust it to do its job. Don't be too hung up on the outcome, but focus more on the present. When we have trust, we relax. When we don't, we are fearful and that will not help our body to heal.

"Self-trust is the first secret of success"
Ralph Waldo Emerson (American poet, philosopher and essayist)

LEARN TO LET GO

I believe we do shape our future by how we think and how we feel, so it goes without saying that I believe that we can create health or ill-health by how we think and feel. This is not to start a blame game as there are many external contributors as well, such as environmental toxins and emotional traumas, but it is necessary to accept some responsibility for our health and the state of our lives. If we play a part in getting ill, then we can play a part in getting well.

However, things happen to us which are out of our control. Life can throw challenges our way and the important thing then is how we deal with them. When we accept that we are going to be confronted by difficult times in our lives, we can learn to accept things that happen and find ways of coping with them, rather than resisting them.

When I heard that my cancer had returned and that I would probably only live for a few more years, I felt pure, undiluted terror. I was forty-five years old with three fantastic children and a husband I did not want to leave behind. I knew that this was my second and final wake-up call, that I hadn't listened to the first one, and that I had some work to do if I wanted to live. I made a pact with the universe, which I have talked about before. I would do everything I could to get better. I was going to start looking after myself. I would eat nourishing foods, exercise, relax and seek help to sort out my thoughts and emotions. The rest I was going to hand over to the universe, to life itself. I put my trust in it there and then. It was a trust that came from my heart, rather than my mind, and I begged the universe not to let me down.

We all know that too much stress is not good for us but we must remember that it is how we react to events that matters and not the events themselves. This is encouraging, as we can learn to reprogram our thinking and let go of thinking which is negative and limiting. We can learn to stop worrying and to forgive ourselves and others. By putting our trust in a more natural order of things and in our own healing powers, we can be more accepting of things.

Throughout my life I have had, apart from the first few days after my second diagnosis, an unwavering belief in the universe or life itself. I am convinced that by being in the driving seat of my own recovery but also surrendering somewhat, and trusting in the benign force of life, I accelerated my own healing. I have had some incredible instances of synchronicity in my life, which would be impossible to ignore. They have led me to books, people or events which have to be more than coincidental and often they have answered my prayers, sometimes big ones!

Einstein famously said "Coincidence is God's way of remaining anonymous". It doesn't really matter whether you believe in coincidence or synchronicity but try to believe a bit more in life itself and things working out. I have never thought, despite a strong spiritual belief, in sitting back and letting some higher being do the work. I know we have to help ourselves but there are times when a little belief in things working out means that we can off load some of the worries and concerns that come with challenging times. So let go, breathe deeply and go with the flow. There is no point in battling upstream. Divert your attention from illness to health and wellbeing. This is vital. Learning about the disease is good but obsessing about it (which I have done for too long a period) keeps us there. Life is here to support you so tap into life and nourish your joy of it and your will to live.

> *"Those who don't believe in magic will never find it"*
> **Roald Dahl** (British novelist, poet and screenwriter)

OUR MENTAL AND EMOTIONAL HEALTH

There are three aspects to our mental and emotional health that I believe we need to deal with.

1. Learning to deal with stress, especially the stress that accompanies a cancer diagnosis.
2. Learning to find a more positive, optimistic outlook on life.
3. Learning to deal with and release any past emotional trauma that you may still be holding onto.

They are all interlinked and I have already discussed many aspects of them in previous sections, such as dealing with fear, but I will continue with the overall picture here.

Firstly, as we know, a bit of stress can do us no harm and can often be the necessary button to kickstart us into action that we need to take. Long term negative thoughts and emotions though, such as anger, fear, stress and loneliness weaken our immune system, leaving us highly vulnerable to disease by flooding our bodies with stress hormones from the adrenal glands, such as cortisol. As we know, it is not the situations that are in themselves negative or stressful, it is how we react to them which is important. Everyone experiences events in their lives differently. We can be confronted by potentially deeply stressful situations, yet deal with them positively and objectively, seeing them as opportunities rather than limitations. When we are more aware of our thoughts and emotions, we can be more in control of our lives and therefore our healing.

We really do need to try and recognise what causes us stress and then do something about it, whether it be a job, relationship, financial situation or anything else. We need to work out how to change these situations and most of the time, we do have choices. If we really don't, then we have to change how we think about the situations. If we want to get well, we have to have the courage to make some often difficult decisions. Again, go with your gut feeling about this. Which is the right thing to do for your health and general wellbeing?

When our mental health is good, we, for the most part, have good self-esteem, are true to ourselves and take care of ourselves. This means we will, in general, eat well, exercise, relax and be more in touch with our needs. It does not mean we have to be self-obsessed but it does mean we can learn to say no to things that don't serve us and reduce the things and people in our lives which drain us.

When it comes to increasing our positive emotions, it is not possible to be positive all the time, but we can put more importance on feeling good. When we do, good hormones are released into our bloodstream, such as endorphins, serotonin and oxytocin. These hormones have many functions such as lowering blood pressure and cortisol, increasing white blood cell activity, improving blood circulation and removing cancer cells. A positive outlook on life is definitely good for our health. Happiness is a state of mind and something we can learn to achieve.

Inevitably though, we will experience negative feelings, which are natural and part of life. When we do so, we need to allow them (there is no point resisting them even if you can) but we need to know when it's time to move ourselves on to a better place. Focusing on things that make us feel good will shift and raise our energy. When we get stuck moaning, complaining or worrying about things, we do the opposite. We need to break those habits and just think of something or do something that makes us FEEL better. We need to feel acceptance and gratitude for what we have as there is always something to feel grateful or good about, whatever your circumstances. Focusing on that will start shifting things and put you in a completely different place. It works. Meditation is so effective in changing your mood as is exercise or being out in nature.

What we focus on, we will get more of – it is the simple law of attraction. So we need to make sure we are thinking about things we want or love! We really need to stop obsessing so much about this disease, and direct our attention to health, happiness and wellbeing, which isn't all that easy in a system and society which places so much attention and fear on cancer. Instead we can try and start to put our energy into how we live each day, and take the emphasis off the end product, such as being cancer free. Of course we can have these goals, but if we are always focusing on them, we are usually fixated on the fact that we haven't reached that goal yet, and that can make us feel anxious and down. We can become preoccupied and even obsessed with trying to fix the problems and this usually comes from a place of fear.

This is where mindfulness and being fully present in what you are doing is so effective. When we do that, thoughts subside and we feel calmer. We slow down too and notice things we might normally miss, such as the blossom on the trees on the way to work, the smiling stranger or the ridiculous position our dog has gone to sleep in.

We can change our thinking and let go of this attempt to constantly fix things, worrying about what we are doing and whether it is the right thing. FEEL what is right instead and go with what feels empowering. Focus more on creating what you want rather than problem solving.

We need to use our emotions as indicators of how we are doing. When we are feeling good, we are on the right track and will be helping our bodies heal. When we are not, we have to make a bit more effort to change our thoughts so that we do feel better. It is that simple but not always easy. Change your thoughts so that you feel better or get on and do something that will lift your spirits. You can't expect to think a thought that will help you move from feeling dreadful to feeling amazing. I am talking about small steps here. Think of anything that makes you feel better. We have a spring-fed pond at the end of the garden and I imagine summer days spent lying there with my family. My eldest, lazy daughter reading a book in a rubber dingy, my youngest son and his best friend leaping about in it, screaming because it is SO cold, and my middle daughter sucking her thumb and lying in the sun beside it. My husband, of course, is asleep in a deckchair, snoring. It makes me smile, relax and feel good. In reality, at this moment, the pond is the colour of pea soup and suffering from an algae problem, it is raining and the dingy has got a puncture!

Find something to be grateful for – having a roof over your head, having a comfortable bed, having a good friend. Make the effort to think of something or visualise a scene. Imagine the people you love and being with them, doing something you love – a past memory or a completely imagined scene. The longer you can sit and imagine these things, the stronger the shift you will feel to a better place. Learn to be content and make peace with the past.

Remember, that how you live each day is helping create your future. Breaking old habits of thinking is hard, but it is possible. It is like exercising a muscle – the more you do it, the easier and more sustained it becomes. As doing so begins to change your life (it does), it becomes easier as you begin to feel more joy and magic in your life. You can do this. Put your attention to who and what you love, and remember to include yourself in that. Learning to love and accept yourself for who you are is the key to a healthy mind.

As far as learning to release negative emotions that you are holding onto from the past, everyone will find different ways to do this. The key is to give yourself some time and space to do so. Often getting away from your day to day life for a bit is important to work it all out and allow negative emotions to flow again. When they get stuck, they can become toxic for us. For me, I have found that Emotional Freedom Technique (EFT) and the Emotion Code work of Dr Bradley Nelson have been incredible at releasing suppressed emotions and dealing with tricky issues, which were holding me back. I can't recommend them highly enough. I have taught myself EFT by researching and watching videos online, and happened to find a fantastic Emotion Code therapist near me, although it was all done by Skype so it is possible to have a session wherever you live. There are so many different types of energy medicine and energy clearing/balancing therapies out there. You really don't have to believe in anything, but just be open-minded. They can often shift things way faster than talking therapies can.

Another therapy to help release negative emotions is EMDR (eye movement desensitization and reprocessing), which seems to work best for buried trauma that you can't necessarily remember. Find a therapist or a healer. Many people have talked of meditation retreats (including silent ones) as being life-changing. Another method, which many people have spoken highly about is that of 'radical forgiveness', devised by Colin Tipping. He offers a different way of looking at events or people who have hurt us, and helps us overcome the victim archetype. His book, 'Radical Forgiveness' is worth reading and his techniques are really quite simple, and from my research there seems to be quite a link between cancer and the need for forgiveness (of others and oneself).

I became interested in the story of Brenda Cobb about a year ago, through an article I had read. In 1999 she was diagnosed with breast and cervical cancer and given around six months to live. Much to the annoyance of her oncologist she refused any conventional treatment as she had watched numerous members of her family be diagnosed with cancer, undergo conventional treatment and then die. I spoke to her on the phone when I was needing some guidance and courage and she said how she remembers going into a bookshop on her way out from the oncologist, and asking if they had any books on how to heal cancer naturally. They did have just one (back then the idea of healing cancer naturally was a new concept) and so she began to take advice from the book and eat organic, raw, vegan food and clear out and heal all the emotional baggage she felt she was carrying with the help of a therapist and her own belief and courage.

Six months after her diagnosis she was healed, with no sign of cancer in her body. She now runs the Living Foods Institute in Atlanta (from which I have recently returned) and teaches people how to heal their bodies from any disease through nutrition, detox and emotional healing, with remarkable results. When I spoke to her, she put healing down to six steps in this order of importance: mental thinking, healing the emotional self, dealing with stress, detoxing, nutrition and supplements/essential oils. Nutrition and detoxing can really speed up healing time but our mental and emotional health is the key to a full recovery. She mentioned tapping as a way to heal the emotional self and that it can work for everyone but that you need to stop believing it is too simple and 'won't work for me'. She also mentions Colin Tipping's book on forgiveness. What struck me when talking to her was her 'bloody mindedness' and determination to open up our minds to the truth – that cancer, like all other diseases, is reversible and just requires us to start believing that and then take the steps needed to find health and wellbeing again.

'You must find the place inside yourself where nothing is impossible'
Deepak Chopra

GET TAPPING

'Emotional Freedom Technique' (EFT) was developed in the 1990s by Gary Craig, a Stanford engineering graduate, who specialised in healing and self-improvement, although it has evolved from acupressure, so its foundations go way back. It falls under the umbrella of Energy Medicine and has only more recently been backed up by scientific research. It seems to be having incredible results on people and to be one of the simplest, fastest and most effective techniques available to us to get rid of pain, heal past events and deal with any stress we are experiencing. It seems that EFT is the tool we can use to change anything in our lives, and it is both simple and effective. I fully admit I found the idea of it a little too straightforward and cranky to start with.

 EFT involves tapping on the end points of meridians in the body, whilst saying certain statements and focusing on the problem. You then gradually move on to positive statements. You always open by tapping on the side of a your hand (fist shaped) as you say the main statement, which starts 'even though I have this……..'. You insert the problem or issue here, such as 'anger about' or 'fear of' or 'difficulty sleeping'. Then you finish the statement with 'I deeply love and accept myself'. That is the hardest bit for most people to do! You then continue to tap on each point while you shorten the statement to just the negative part – 'this stress', 'this fear' and so on. Once you have gone through each point a couple of times, tapping at least seven times on each point, you start to make it more positive. Again, you don't have to say full sentences but you would expand here a bit. For example, if you were talking about the fear you aren't getting well, you might say things like 'I know my body is strong', 'I know my body knows exactly what to do',' I just need to relax and breathe' and gradually get more positive. You get better with practice and the right words just begin to flow naturally.

 It can feel weird to do it but quite frankly you will get over that when you research the results and hype around it, and start noticing the benefits yourself. The more specific you can be about the issue, the better. Research shows that when we tap, we send calming messages to the amygdala, which is the 'fight or flight' response centre of our brain. The production of cortisol is greatly reduced, along with the distress we experience. Our brains are being rewired and bringing our bodies and minds into balance and it seems our problems simply dissipate. We are shifting and moving energy, which starts to flow freely again in our systems.

I am really new to this but am using it for all sorts of things when I remember to. It is really easy to forget to use it as a tool. From what I have experienced, it is definitely having results, from getting rid of pain to moving emotional blocks and feelings of confusion, frustration and self-doubt. I have spoken to someone who was very ill with Crohn's disease, and who had tried several things including changing his diet to a much healthier one. He believed he had underlying emotional trauma which needed to be dealt with and had heard of EFT. He tried an EFT practitioner and said it was life-changing and healed his disease. From testimonials from respected practitioners and other health experts, it seems it is capable of changing anything in your life, whether that be creating more meaningful relationships, wealth or great health. It seems it can break the patterns that have been holding us back for so long and although it may seem weird and too good to be true, it has to be worth a try. I suggest you go to www.tappingsolutions.com as a way in to this technique.

ENERGY - THE MEDICINE OF THE FUTURE?

I have always had a strong belief in something greater than ourselves, something mystical and magical that can potentially create miracles. I have just felt it as a presence ever since I can remember, and it has always been a part of my life. I have definitely remained in the spiritual closet though, as it is a domain that has seen a lot of bad press (sometimes deservedly) and quite frankly often seems to require that we take life too seriously. How can one prove something that you can't see, touch, hear, smell or taste to those who need evidence of its existence?

Just before my first diagnosis, I was really preoccupied with my daughters' schooling. They were at our local school but the younger one, who was five years old and very quiet, wasn't happy. My bright, energetic eldest daughter was not really engaged. She was bored. I knew of a small, creative private school nearby that I wanted them to go to. It was run by a brilliant, somewhat eccentric and creative woman, who was the sort of role model I wanted my daughters to have. She was strong-willed, spoke her mind and was non-conformist. I knew my children would thrive there but we couldn't afford it, especially now we had a two year old son as well. I remember walking the dog in the fields behind the house. I was down and angry and can't remember why, but I do remember shouting at the skies. I screamed that I was fed up of doing my best, of caring about and giving generously to the world, yet continuing to feel hopeless and lost. My complete obsession was with the children and how we were going to give them a stimulating, happy education and I finished my tirade by giving the universe an ultimatum – 'give me a sign that you are listening or I am giving up on you'. The very next day I received a phone call that made sending all three children to that school possible for the next four years or so. It would see my girls get to their senior school. I remember putting the phone down in shock as I realised instantly that my message had been received loud and clear, and duly answered.

There is a new science evolving, based on the integration between ancient wisdom and modern science. It seems to prove the existence of an intelligent force at play in the world. The outmoded idea that we react to events in our life which we have no control over can be replaced by the understanding that we can create the life we want and manifest change. There are a growing number of authors, researchers, psychologists, doctors and scientists who are discovering that not only are we capable of making changes to our lives but are explaining how we can go about achieving them.

Dr Joe Dispenza is one such person. He has a long list of credentials and I have read his book, "Breaking the Habit of Being Yourself", which has its foundations in Quantum physics. In it he explains that mind and matter (which is really just energy or frequency patterns of information) are completely interlinked, and that the energy becomes matter (something) only when the subjective mind focuses upon it. He explains that we are part of a huge, invisible field of energy (the quantum field), in which all possible realities exist and which responds to our thoughts and feelings. This quantum field, however, will only respond when both our wishes (our emotional requests) and our thoughts (aims) are aligned or on the same frequency.

In other words, our wishes can come true not in response to our desires but in response to who we are being. By this he means that "when you hold clear, focused thoughts about your purpose, accompanied by your passionate emotional engagement, you broadcast a stronger electromagnetic signal that pulls you toward a potential reality that matches what you want". (11)

Thoughts are the language of the brain and feelings the language of the body, so if you think healthy thoughts, for example, but you are aware of the current reality of your health/body and feeling a lack of health, you can't attract good health for yourself. So we shouldn't sit and wait for something to happen to give us the emotional experience we want. We can actually make it happen by thinking it and feeling how it feels to have it BEFORE it actually happens. I have over-simplified this but look at Dispenza's website (www.drjoedispenza.com) and read the testimonials about what people have managed to bring into existence, including healing themselves. The tool he uses and teaches to achieve change is meditation and he shows us how to do his particular type of meditation in the book.

Lynne Taggart is another award-winning author, journalist and editor of one of the world's leading health magazines "What doctors don't tell you." She has done in-depth research into our ability to create what we want, especially her ground-breaking work into the power of intention, which, as a form of thought, is just another form of energy. She is a leading authority on this new science and is proving that thoughts have the capacity to change physical matter. She is conducting the 'Intention Experiment' involving prestigious scientists and readers in ongoing experiments of small groups, where her techniques create major changes in the brain, leading to profound changes and life-long transformations in people's lives. Her techniques seem to be having a profound effect on many people and anyone can partake in them.

Gregg Braden is another author and scientist best known for his book 'The Divine Matrix'. He was diagnosed in 2000 with a tumour that he was told needed immediate surgery to remove it. He asked for two weeks, during which he applied his extensive knowledge in this area, and of course when they opened him up to remove it, it had vanished. He says that without doubt, the cells in our bodies are constantly healing and repairing themselves and that we just need to step out of the way and let them get on with it.

So it seems there is a new science evolving which is beginning to explain the powerful life force that exists within us all. This life force is energy and is intelligent. It runs through us and we all have access to it. Although ancient wisdom has always known about it (acupuncture has recognised the existence of energy meridians for thousands of years), there is definitely some momentum gathering in our willingness to open our minds more and accept the existence of an intelligent life force to which we are all connected, and a willingness to explore the unknown and its potential.

Scientific research is proving that we are beings of energy and is recognizing the healing power of certain therapies such as acupuncture and kinesiology. A door has been opened with the discoveries of quantum physics and the acceptance that everything is energy. Energy Medicine is, I believe, the medicine of the future. These therapies, such as EFT, Reiki, Kinesiology, Reflexology and energy healing all work by shifting energy and clearing blockages in our energy system which enable our bodies to be brought back into balance and harmony. What is more, we can teach ourselves how to balance our own bodies and energy systems. It is simple and user friendly, and there are courses (including online ones) everywhere. Donna Eden is one of the big names if you want to look into this more, and I am doing one of her online courses at the moment (www.innersource.net).

I have also recently finished a weekend course on pure bioenergy healing in London, where I witnessed severe pain disappear in less than three minutes of treatment. One could feel anything between warmth and tingling sensations to distinct movements in our bodies when being given healing, and this was just between students learning the techniques. It involves channeling energy through one's hands to different points of the body. The stories of healing, often after only one or two sessions, were quite astonishing. All manner of illnesses and problems have had success with this simple energy healing, from severe allergies, diabetes, cancer to depression and autism.

You don't have to believe in this life force (energy) to benefit from it, even though its existence has been recognised by sages and scientists for a very long time. The Hindus called it Prana, the Chinese called it Chi and many know it as Bioenergy. It can be used for any illness, injury, ongoing problem as well as stress, anxiety and depression. Anything and everything. We know that mobile phones, radio and televisions all work using frequencies. We cannot see these frequencies but we know they exist, even if we don't entirely understand how they work. Energy medicine is similar. Energy healing occurs when the energy, which contains the information needed, creates changes needed for the body to heal. The frequency is the information and the body is able to understand the communication being provided. I would just say try to be open-minded rather than resistant to all this, and know that there are things we maybe cannot explain or understand entirely but that we can still be open to the fact that our bodies and minds are capable of great things.

'Problems of this world cannot be solved by cynics and skeptics but by people with vision, confidence and hope'
George Bernard Shaw (Irish playwright)

KEEP YOUR SENSE OF HUMOUR

The cancer journey unfolds organically, in terms of how we respond emotionally. It tends to move through different stages with ups and downs throughout, usually starting with shock and fear. There are plenty of times when it is just so hard, but we sometimes need reminding too, not to take it all too seriously. We are all going to die, we are all 'terminal', and none of us know when that will be. So, we mustn't get so immersed in the bubble we find ourselves in, when dealing with cancer, that we forget to enjoy life and just have some fun. It is vital to all of us and extremely good for our health.

I have one particular friend who I can't be with for very long before we are laughing. Being around her lifts me up every time. However, if you don't have a 'funny friend' at hand, then watch some comedies, ridiculous YouTube videos (my children have plenty they can show me), put on some uplifting music or read an amusing book. It's all good stuff and shifts things quickly. I realise that the content of this book can seem quite intense and really advocates finding some stillness and peace in our crazy lives, so that we can think straight, listen to our inner voice and find a way through challenging times, but a sense of humour is something we should keep with us. We may just need to remind ourselves now and then to 'lighten up' and have some fun.

"A good laugh overcomes more difficulties and dissipates more dark clouds than any other one thing"
Laura Ingalls Wilder (American Writer)

AND FINALLY...

The world is more medically and technologically advanced than ever, yet there is more sickness in our world too. Our lives are getting busier and busier, and for the most part we have lost the ability to recognise that what we have mostly accepted as 'the norm', doesn't need to be and isn't really serving us. It is not only in Western society but gradually in all industrialised, developed societies that being busy, stressed and anxious is what we expect of ourselves and others. We are mostly overloaded with choices, our heads scrambled with information, and often on a treadmill, going nowhere. I feel that many of us have lost the connection with ourselves, with others and with the life force that runs to us and through us. I know I had.

However, there is definitely a shift going on, as many of us search for more meaning to this life and begin to realise that we can choose to experience it differently, if we can just find the courage to change things so that we start living the life we truly want to live. If we can open our hearts and minds more, we can start to realise that we are only just scratching at the surface of the huge potential out there in terms of healing our physical bodies, our lives in general and the world at large. We just need a different way of thinking, to move beyond our conditioned minds to a greater awareness of both ourselves and the world around us.

Modern medicine is becoming more personalised, which is a good thing but is still missing the point, focusing on the cure and not the cause. External remedies to our health don't have the lasting or powerful results that internal ones do. Until we tend to the individual person, i.e our whole health, we cannot really heal. We know there is a link between our emotions and cancer and it is now accepted that stress is a major contributor to cancer but we still don't place enough importance on these links. Even if we did, the fact is we can't treat our emotional health with drugs. As William Osier, often called the 'father of modern medicine' said, "it is much more important to know what sort of patient has a disease than what sort of disease a patient has".

We cannot depend on doctors to sort out our mental and emotional health. We can use the help of anything and anyone, but we need to find the courage to discover our own way to health by going within and gaining greater self-awareness. People are beginning to do this and be in the driving seat of their recovery, finding ways to support themselves, but it isn't easy to do this in a system that promotes fear, mystery and often hopelessness around the subject of cancer.

The more we put the spotlight on illness, the more we think about it and the problems it brings. Most of the statistics, news and information about the illness just feeds our stress, our anxieties and our fear. We get so hung up on the illness and trying to fight it that we forget how to live. Yet this is exactly where we have to place our emphasis…on LIVING. We must remember the importance of the moment, of today. When our minds are preoccupied by the past or what the future holds, we miss the freshness of the present moment. By completely accepting where we are now and making peace with it, we are able to move forward. We can start taking small steps with happy feet or quantum leaps, whichever we can manage, but small steps are fine.

What we lose track of in our search for a greater meaning to and understanding of this life, is that it all starts with a greater understanding and acceptance of who we are. When we get to know, love and accept ourselves, we start to take more responsibility for ourselves and our lives. We start to shift our beliefs about our own limitations and powerlessness and realise that anything is possible. This belief feeds our sense of vitality and feelings about life being worth living. As we learn to love ourselves more, we are able to love others more and give more to the world. We have to start with ourselves. Love is so healing and gives our life meaning. When our lives have meaning, we are connected to that life force. Energy starts to flow again, and we feel energised and full of vitality and excitement about the lives we are living and the world we are living in.

Cancer has led me to go on a journey within. I know it was asking me to start living a life that was in alignment with who I really am. It was asking that I say what I truly wanted to say and live by my own values without fear of being judged or alienated. Throughout my life I have felt out on a limb, desperately wanting to help mend a broken world yet feeling that I was in the wrong place at the wrong time. What I have learnt is that I wasn't able to give anything until I had first given to myself...filled up my glass if you like and tended to my needs. I needed to stop beating myself up about everything and just be myself and open my eyes to the beauty and perfection that was in my life already. I needed to stop looking outside of me at the problems and focus instead on feeling good. I never placed enough value on my emotions but instead put my energy into action, and then beat myself up when this was never good enough.

This journey inward wasn't self-indulgent, as I would previously have thought, but necessary in order to wake up and smell the roses. I never knew life could be so rich and meaningful, and that I could feel so much positive anticipation about what is to come. I don't see a broken world anymore, even though that is all we see and hear in the news. I see a beautiful world full of variation – with many more good people and things happening than we hear about. It all depends where you look. There is always going to be pain and sorrow. It is part of life but often we just need to be more accepting of this and move on from it when we feel the time is right. We can all give and help those in need more but we must remember to give to ourselves too.

I have been lucky to have such loving support from my family and friends but it is a lonely journey at times. I couldn't have got through those lonely, dark moments without the help of life itself, which is what connects us all and makes our lives beautiful. Have more trust in it supporting you. The more you relax and trust, the more it will reveal itself to you.

There is no doubt in my mind that these 'hiccups' are just reminders that we still have much to learn, and that if we can accept the challenge and make some changes, we can awaken our own lives and then the lives of others. It is the ripple effect, and by changing our own lives, we can change the world. Simple, eh? Have courage, believe in yourself and life and get happy. Go slow, with gratitude and love, for yourself and others, and focus on each day at a time. You will find your way through.

A FEW THINGS TO REMEMBER

1. WHAT YOU PUT YOUR ATTENTION TO, YOU GET MORE OF – so make sure you are focusing on good things.

2. BREATHE – deeply and slowly every day.

3. WORDS HAVE POWER – think about how you speak and the words you use. Surround yourself with quotes, affirmations and words that make you feel good, and speak them too.

4. REST AND RELAX – physically, mentally and emotionally. Know when your body needs rest, and learn to relax and let go of worries and stresses.

5. BE GRATEFUL – it is the starting point for making you feel better about things. Look at the things in your life and the world that work and that you love – there are plenty of them.

6. SEE FOOD AS NOURISHING YOUR BODY – and be more mindful of how and what you eat. Make eating healthily enjoyable rather than a chore.

7. STOP COMPLAINING – it helps nobody. Least of all yourself.

8. GET OUTSIDE – and appreciate the natural world, even if it is your local park. Watch the seasons come and go, grow something beautiful or that you can eat!

9. LEARN TO LET GO – of those worries and irritations. Go with the flow more – life becomes easier when you do. Worrying is pointless – always. Trust instead.

10. WHEN YOU ARE FEELING FRANTIC AND OVERWHELMED – this is the time to stop, breathe and bring yourself back to the present!

11. BE KIND – to yourself and others. We are all just doing what we can.

12. IT WILL PASS – however bad things seem, remember that everything is transitory. Relax, let go more and things will eventually change.

TWO WOLVES

A Cherokee Proverb

An old Cherokee told his grandson:

'My son, there is a battle between two wolves inside us all. One is evil. It is anger, envy, jealousy, sorrow, regret, greed, arrogance, self-pity, guilt, resentment, inferiority, lies, false pride, superiority and ego.

The other is good. It is joy, peace, love, hope, serenity, humility, kindness, benevolence, generosity, empathy and truth.'

The grandson thought about this for a minute and then asked his grandfather, 'Which wolf wins?'

The old Cherokee simply replied…'the one you feed.'

RESOURCES

BOOKS

Anti-Cancer: A New Way of Life by David Servan-Schreiber- Penguin books, Paris 2007

Breaking the Habit of Being Yourself by Dr Joe Dispenza – Hay House 2012

Radical Forgiveness by Colin Tipping – Sounds True Inc, Canada 2009

Radical Remission by Kelly A. Turner – HarperCollins 2015

How Not To Die by Michael Greger, MD – Pan Macmillan, UK 2016

Digestive Solutions by Michele Wolff – Global Publishing Group, Australia 2013

Crazy Sexy Diet by Kris Carr – Skirt!, US 2011

Dying To Be Me by Anita Moorjani – Hay House 2012

Love, Medicine and Miracles by Bernie S. Siegel – Rider, GB 1986

The Rainbow Diet by Chris Woollams – Health Issues Ltd, UK 2008

Women's Bodies, Women's Wisdom by Dr Christiane Northrup – Piatkus Books Ltd, London 1995

Cancer-Free, Your Guide to Gentle, Non-Toxic Healing by Bill Henderson – Booklocker.com 2008

Clean – The Revolutionary Program to Restore the Body's Natural Ability to Heal Itself by Alejandro Junger, M.D. – HarperCollins, U.S. 2009

The Emotion Code by Dr Bradley Nelson – Wellness Unmasked Publishing 2007

The Ultimate Happiness Prescription by Deepak Chopra – Ebury Publishing 2010

USEFUL CONTACTS

www.maggiescentres.org These amazing centres offer practical, emotional and social support to cancer patients, their families and friends.

www.pennybrohncancercare.org The Penny Brohn Cancer Centre is the UK's leading holistic cancer charity and runs various courses. I went on a weekend course there (they just ask for a donation) early after my second diagnosis. I would highly recommend it and they are just outside Bristol.

www.chrisbeatcancer.com - you can find plenty of advice on nutrition and natural therapies from Chris Wark who was diagnosed with stage 3 colon cancer at the age of 26. He refused chemo and is healthy and cancer free fourteen years later.

www.canceractive.com - set up by Chris Woollams who lost his daughter to cancer.

www.nutritionfacts.org - a non-profit site set up by Michael Greger, MD and is full of the latest in evidence-based nutrition.

www.thehaven.org.uk - this charity provides emotional, physical and practical support for breast cancer patients.

www.bodysoulnutrition.co.uk - this team of cancer experts and nutritionists provide much more than advice on nutrition and supplements. They have a body/mind/soul approach to cancer.

www.findyourinnerharmony.co.uk – Amanda Brooks is an amazing lady who is trained, amongst many things, to do the Emotion Code work (releasing trapped emotions). She can do remote work too so it doesn't matter where you live.

www.healthycolon.co.uk – Ann Knott is a naturopath, colonic hydrotherapist and quantum therapist, who uses the quantum scio test to discover individual needs in terms of diet, vitamins and minerals.

BY KIND PERMISSION OF KRIS CARR 'CRAZY, SEXY DIET'

PLANT FOODS HIGH IN PROTEIN

Food	Amount	Protein in grams
Almonds	¼ Cup	7.4
Barley, Pearled	½ Cup	3.6
Black Beans	1 Cup	15
Black-Eyes Peas	1 Cup	13
Broccoli	1 Cup, CKD	5
Brown Rice	1 Cup, CKD	9
Cashews	¼ Cup	5
Chickpeas	1 Cup	15
Corn	1 Cup	5
Cranberry Beans	1 Cup	17
Flaxseeds	2 T	4
Hemp Seeds	3 T	15
Kale	1 Cup, CKD	2
Kidney Beans	1 Cup	15
Lentils	1 Cup	18
Lima Beans	1 Cup	15
Millet	1 Cup	8
Natto	½ Cup	15
Navy Beans	1 Cup	16
Oatmeal	1 Cup, CKD	6
Peas	1 Cup	9
Peanut Butter	2 T	7
Peanuts	1 Ounce	7
Pinto Beans	1 Cup	14
Potato, Baked	1 Medium	4
Quinoa	1 Cup, CKD	6
Spinich	1 Cup, CKD	5
Sunflower Seeds	1 Ounce	6
Sweet Potato, Baked	1 Medium	2
Tempah	1 Cup	30
Tofo, Firm	4 Ounces	10
Walnuts	1 Ounce	4

PLANT FOODS HIGH IN CALCIUM

Food	Amount	Calcium in mg
Almonds, Dry-Roasted	1 Ounce	80
Arugula	½ Cup	16
Black Beans	1 Cup	60
Broccoli, Cooked	1 Cup	42
Cabbage, Cooked	½ Cup	35
Chickpeas	1 Cup	80
Collard Greens, Cooked	½ Cup	113
Cranberry Beans	1 Cup	89
Flaxseeds	1 Ounce	48
Kale, Cooked	½ Cup	90
Kidney Beans	1 Cup	50
Lentils	1 Cup	38
Natto	½ Cup	190
Navy Beans	1 Cup	128
Okra	½ Cup	50
Peanuts	1 Ounce	15
Pinto Beans	1 Cup	82
Potato, Baked	1 Medium	20
Quinoa	1 Cup	102
Spinich, Cooked	½ Cup, Raw	30*
Sunflower Seeds	1 Ounce	34
Sweet Potato, Baked	1 Medium	32
Swiss Chard, Cooked	½ Cup	30*
Tahini	1 Ounce	128
Tempah	1 Cup	184
Tofu	½ Cup	130
Turnip Greens, Cooked	½ Cup	99

TOP ALKALINE FOODS (eat as many as you want)	ACIDIC FOODS RUNDOWN (eat in moderation or not at all)
Alkaline Water.	Alcohol.
Almonds, brazil nuts, sesame seeds, and flaxseeds.	Animal protein: red meat, poultry, fish, eggs, milk, cheese, dairy products (these products are highly acidic)
Avocados.	Chemicals, drugs, cigs, heavy metals, pesticides, preservatives.
Cold-pressed oils such as hemp, flax, and borage seeds.	Coffee (even decaf), black tea.
Moderate amounts of grains such as quinoa, wild rice, millet, amaranth, buck wheat. Exceptions: wheat, oats and brown rice are mildly acidic.	Heavily processed foods, no matter what they are made of.
Grasses, especially superpowered nutrient-packed wheatgrass.	Honey, corn syrup, brown sugar, fructose.
Green drinks.	Ketchup, Mayonnaise and Mustard.
Green veggies – all kinds, but especially leafy green veggies such as kale, spinach, lettuces, collards, mustard greens, turnip greens, cabbage and endive.	Some legumes like chickpeas, black beans, and soybeans are slightly acidic but are valuable staples of a healthy diet.
Lemons, limes and grapefruits – although these fruits are acidic, they actually have an alkalizing affect in your body.	Processed soy products tend to fall on the acidic side – enjoy them in moderation.
	MSG.
Lentils and other beans – in general, all legumes (beans and peas) are alkalizing.	Processed oils such as margarine, fake fats, trans fats and refined vegetable oils.
Miso.	Refined grains, wheat, and oats: White bread, pasta, and rice are highly acidic.
Oil-cured olives.	Soda, energy drinks and sport drinks.
Raw tomatoes – but cooked tomatoes are acidic.	Table salt (sea salt and kosher salt are better choices in moderation)
Root veggies, such as sweet potatoes, potatoes, turnips, daikon and burdock.	All salted and roasted nuts.
Seaweed.	White sugar and sugar substitutes.
Sprouts.	Yeast and vinegar (except for raw apple cider vinegar), soy sauce (use sparingly and choose low sodium tamari or gluten-free nama shoyu.
Stevia (a sweetener)	

DIRTY FOODS	CLEAN FOODS
Foods grown with the most pesticides, ranked from worst to less bad.	Foods grown with the least amount of pesticides, ranked from best to not-so-good.
1. Peach 2. Apple 3. Bell Pepper 4. Celery 5. Necterine 6. Strawberries 7. Cherries 8. Kale 9. Lettuce 10. Grapes (Imported) 11. Carrot 12. Pear	1. Onion 2. Avocado 3. Sweetcorn 4. Pineapple 5. Mango 6. Asparagus 7. Sweet Peas 8. Kiwi 9. Cabbage 10. Eggplant 11. Papaya 12. Watermelon 13. Broccoli 14. Tomato 15. Sweet Potato

REFERENCES

1. David Hamilton – 'How Your Mind Can Heal Your Body' p. 40

2. Anita Moorjani – 'Dying To Be Me' p. 50

3. Kris Carr – 'Crazy, Sexy Diet' – p. 72

4. Kris Carr – 'Crazy, Sexy Diet' – p. 23

5. Tony Isaacs – 'Our Disappearing Minerals and their Vital Health' 14/05/2008 www.naturalnews.com

6. Frank Lipman – 'Crazy, Sexy Diet' p. 171

7. David. R Hamilton – 'How Your Mind Can Heal Your Body' p. 86

8. Dr David Servan-Schreiber – 'anti- cancer – a new way of life' p. 226

9. Dr David Servan-Schreiber – 'anti-cancer – a new way of life' p. 226

10. Bernie Siegel – 'Love, Medicine and Miracles' p. 82

11. Dr Joe Dispenza – 'Breaking the Habit of Being Yourself' p. 23

RECIPES

I am including some of my own favourite recipes here. The quantities are a rough guide but should feed 4 people. All vegan but not all suitable for a ketogenic diet.

Grapefruit and rocket salad - add the segments of 2 red grapefruits (or any grapefruit) to 4 handfuls of rocket. Toast some pine nuts and add them to the salad plus a sliced avocado. Add the dressing. To make this add these ingredients but adjust the quantities to your own taste. I use about one-third cider vinegar to two-thirds extra virgin olive oil. Add a tablespoon of Dijon mustard and a squirt of agave or maple syrup to sweeten.

Wild rice, rocket and pomegranate salad - cook 200g of wild rice and leave to cool slightly. Add 4 handfuls of rocket and the seeds of 1 or preferably 2 pomegranates. You can choose to add some shredded cooked chicken if eating meat. Add the same dressing as above and be generous.

Quinoa risottos – quinoa is a great source of protein and gluten free. The key is not to overcook it, so these recipes don't take long to cook. Always start softening a large onion and 2 or 3 cloves of garlic in some butter or coconut oil, depending on your taste. Then…

> Spring risotto – add courgettes and cook for a couple of minutes. Add the quinoa and mix into the onion mix. After a couple of minutes add some good stock (ideally homemade chicken stock or good quality cubes/bouillon). Keep stirring and then add some chopped mint, peas, and broad beans. I sometimes add broccoli and/or asparagus which I have pre-steamed. Just don't

overcook them. Lots of pepper and some Himalayan salt.

Beetroot risotto – bake or boil some beetroot in its skin. Cool and peel away the skin and chop up. Sweat the onion and garlic, add the quinoa and stock and cook. Add more stock as necessary and when it is cooked and has soaked up all the stock, season well and add the chopped beetroot and plenty of chopped parsley. I usually crumble a bit of feta cheese on the top for my family or even mix in a tablespoon of mascarpone cheese.

Spinach risotto – add some grated nutmeg to the sweated onion and garlic. Towards the end, mix in plenty of shredded spinach or baby spinach. Make sure there is plenty of seasoning.

<u>Quinoa tabbouleh </u>- cook the quinoa according to instructions but make sure you cook slowly and don't overcook it, otherwise it is too stodgy and congealed. Chop up 5 or 6 large tomatoes and add to the quinoa once it is cooled. Chop lots of mint and parsley and add to the mixture, and season well with salt and pepper. For the dressing – squeeze the juice of 2 lemons and add some chopped/pressed garlic (optional). Add a pinch of cinnamon and then some olive oil. It should be about a third lemon juice to two thirds olive oil.

<u>Asian rice and seaweed salad</u> - cook some brown basmati or brown rice and leave to cool. It is nice to eat this when the rice is still a little warm. Grate 2 courgettes and add to the cooled rice and along with 1 or 2 chopped red peppers. Toast some nori seaweed sheets (put on a frying pan with no oil…sometimes I don't bother toasting) and then shred into small pieces and add to the rice. Toast some sesame seeds to add on top once dressed. For the dressing – grate a generous thumb of ginger into a bowl. Add some tamari sauce (2 large tbspoons) and a squirt of agave or maple syrup. Then add some toasted sesame oil or olive oil if you

don't have sesame. Adjust to taste but be generous with the dressing and pour over the rice and toss.

Asian broth – homemade chicken stock is way better than stock cubes for this and try and get into the habit of making stock often. Visit a local butcher to ask for left over bones, wings etc. Prepare some vegetables beforehand. I use red peppers, grated carrot, spinach, pak choi or other greens and beansprouts but you can vary them according to taste. Fry some garlic with some onion or spring onion. Add a good teaspoon of red thai curry paste and some grated ginger. Add the stock, the vegetables (in order of which will cook longest) and some rice noodles. Then add a tin of coconut milk and some tamari sauce. Cook it all for a couple of minutes, or until the noodles are cooked. Add a squeeze of lime juice at the end if you want.

Vietnamese rolls- buy some spring roll wrappers/Vietnamese roll wrappers. You need to place each one in a large bowl of boiled water and then carefully take it out, making sure it doesn't wrinkle up. Place it flat on a board and then add some fresh ingredients. I use shredded or baby spinach, fresh mint, thinly sliced red pepper, cucumber and carrots. The mint is really important and you can use any combination of the above, and maybe some coriander or basil. Then make the dipping sauce. Put 2 tablespoons of tamari sauce in a small bowl. Add a tiny squirt of agave sauce to sweeten and then add a glug of sesame oil or olive oil. Adjust to taste. These rolls are delicious and so fresh tasting.

Fabulous Salads - I eat a lot of salads. The key is to make a really good dressing and to add a large variety of vegetables, herbs and seeds etc. Try and make sure you have at least 6 ingredients in the salad. Remember that bitter leaves (rocket, endive, dandelion e.t.c) are really good for you.

In order to make it more tasty and nutritious, use a blender to blend the more hardcore greens such as broccoli, courgette or kale. I tend to blend a couple of carrots and then some broccoli or courgette and add that to the base salad leaves. Blending is helping your digestive system too, making its job easier.

Here are a list of suggestions to add to your salad; leaves, herbs (coriander, basil, mint), sunflower or pumpkin seeds (soaked first for an hour or so), blended green veg and carrot, avocado, tomatoes, cucumber, fennel, peppers, asparagus, cabbage (blended first), sprouts of any sort, flowers (most flowers from the garden are edible and I use them lots to make a salad more attractive) and pulses (e.g. chickpeas, lentils, cannelloni beans). Some cooked quinoa can really improve a salad especially if you add it to blended green veg.

Be generous with your dressing – either use the same dressing as in the first two recipes or a tahini dressing. To make this, use a generous teaspoon of tahini. Add the juice of 2 lemons and a small squirt of tamari sauce plus a tiny amount of agave, raw honey or maple syrup.

Rejuvelac – (fermented cabbage juice). Wierdly I think this tastes good and so does my daughter. It doesn't smell great but is so easy to make and fantastic for your gut health.

Measure one cup of cabbage (white or red but organic) and blend in blender until really smooth. Add 3 cups of water to the blender and blend more. Pour the cabbage mixture into a large glass jar (those pickling jars you get in a hardware shop or online) and make sure you have at least an inch from the top of the jar (allowing room for the gas during the fermentation process). Leave for 72 hours at room temperature to ferment. Then sieve the liquid and discard the cabbage bits (I do this through a muslin or sprouting bag so I can squeeze all the liquid out of the cabbage). Store in a fridge for up to a week and drink a glass or half a glass a day.

(Recipe by kind permission of Brenda Cobb, founder of Living Foods Institute, Atlanta)

Vege-kraut – a low-salt sauerkraut, which is packed with enzymes, aids digestion and helps cleanse our blood.

You need: half a cabbage (red or white), 2 tablespoons juniper berries finely ground in a vita-mix or coffee grinder, 1 teaspoon of Himalayan salt and 2 tablespoons of dulse flakes.

Shred the cabbage finely until the juices are flowing when you squeeze it in your fingers. Add the salt, ground juniper berries and dulse flakes and mix together. Push the mixture into a jar, pushing it down firmly and cover with an outer leaf of cabbage at the top. Put a weight of some sort at the top. Close the lid and leave for 6 days before eating. This will last 6 months in the fridge. Ideally make this in a special fermenting jar, easy to buy online or in a hardware shop. You can make it in any large, glass jar but must leave a bit of air at the top (an inch or so) and then remember to open the lid twice a day to let out the gas as it ferments. It i much easier to buy a fermenting jar or kit..

Really easy to make and you can experiment with different vegetables (carrots, broccoli and cauliflower).

(Recipe by kind permission of Brenda Cobb, founder of Living Foods Institute, Atlanta)

Berry Panna cotta – all you need is some coconut milk (the cartons you buy in any supermarket), some good quality gelatine (I buy vegan gelatine from a health shop), chia seeds and some berries (frozen or fresh).

Follow instructions on the gelatine packet, heating about a pint of milk with 1 teaspoon of gelatine. Let it cool down. Meanwhile whizz up some fresh or frozen (defrosted) berries and add a date or some stevia/agave/maple syrup to sweeten a bit. Pour the milk into ramekins or glasses and put in the fridge to set for half an hour or so. Then add the berry mixture on top and sprinkle with chia seeds when you serve. Easy and delicious. I do about two-thirds panna cotta to one-third berry mixture.